The gourmet's guide to FRENCH COOKING

The gourmet's guide to
FRENCH COOKING
by Alison Burt

TREASURE PRESS

First published by Octopus Books Limited
This edition published by Treasure Press
59 Grosvenor Street
London W1

© 1973 Octopus Books Limited
ISBN 0 907407 43 9
Printed in Hong Kong

this page : Mediterranean vegetable stew
previous page : A selection
of pastries and apple flan

Contents

The flavour of French cooking

French cooking has, quite rightly, earned
itself the reputation of being the finest cuisine
in the world. It is made up of two different parts,
haute cuisine and cuisine bourgeoisie. The former
has evolved from the cooking of the great chefs
such as Escoffier and Câreme. The second is the
peasant cooking of the various regions of France.
You will find both types in this book, so do not
be surprised if you come across a highly
sophisticated dish in company with a simple but
delicious peasant stew.
It is fascinating finding out where the various

dishes of France have originated and how the
local produce has affected the cuisine of each
area. It is particularly useful, if you ever visit
France, to know in advance what to look out for
and the specialities to order in the local
restaurants.
Paris is the political, arts and cooking centre of
France. Every day the best and freshest of
French-grown produce, meat, fruit and vegetables
come into Runjis, near Orly airport, the vast new
market replacing Les Halles. Not only do the shops
and restaurants buy their food here, but also many

A selection of locally produced food

housewives who get up early one or two mornings a week to come to the market for, with true French economy in mind, they know that this is where they will get value for money. It is in the hotels and restaurants of Paris that the great chefs of France have created haute cuisine. Paris is especially noted for its gâteaux and patisserie which are varied, luscious and delicious.

Normandy to the north west of Paris and bordering on the English Channel, is a province of great natural food resources, and many great dishes originated in Normandy. It is an apple growing area and large quantities of very fine cider are made. Dishes which include apples are sometimes called 'à la Normande'. Calvados, the apple-flavoured liqueur, comes from Normandy

and so does Benedictine; the famous Benedictine monastery stands on the cliffs overlooking the sea. A great variety of fish are caught off the coast of Normandy and many shellfish can be gathered from the rocks. Oysters and mussels are especially good and succulent. The dairy industry thrives in Normandy and besides much good quality butter and cream, many of the most famous cheeses come from here. Together with many other regional specialities, Rouen is well known for its ducks and Caen is known for Tripe à la mode de Caen which is sold in that area but now made much in the home.

7

Brittany, just to the south of Normandy, is a peninsula jutting out into the Atlantic ocean. Besides being famed for its oysters, scallops, lobsters and other sea food, this is the home of the salt pastures where the lamb 'pré-sale' is raised. This young and tender lamb has a flavour all of its own which is prized throughout France. Nantes, to the south of Brittany, is a centre for cakes, biscuits and its own version of pike cooked in white wine. Breton charcuterie is well known and its shops sell a wide variety of pâtés, terrines, rillettes, sausages and so on. The autumn in Brittany brings a bountiful harvest of cereals, fruit, vegetables, honey and sweet chestnuts. Incidentally, if you come across a dish in a restaurant called 'à la Breton' it usually means that the meat will be served with a garnish of haricot beans. This has come about because haricot beans are the traditional accompaniment to the Breton gigot de pré-salé (leg of salt-meadow lamb).

The west and the south-west Basque country is rich in vines. Bordeaux is the famed wine centre of this area and it is in this region that Cognac is made. Sea food abounds in the Bay of Biscay and the Gironde estuary can boast of some of the finest caviar from locally caught sturgeons. The Landes province, at the foot of the Pyrenees, can claim many traditional dishes from Pipérade to Cassoulet, both of simple peasant origin. Bayonne is famous for its ham and this area is well-known for locally fattened Landes chickens.

Travelling east along the French border will bring you first to the **Languedoc** and then **Provence.** These two provinces both border on the Mediterranean Sea and the local cuisines are very similar. The climate is good: and fruit flourish. Apricots and peaches are regional specialities and the abundance of herbs help to scent the famous Provence honey. The well known local produce consists of olives (and olive oil), tomatoes, garlic and herbs, and if the words 'à la Provençale' appear on the menu you can be sure that the dish in question will contain at least some of these ingredients. Fish caught in the Mediterranean are naturally part of the local cuisine and it is here that the true Bouillabaisse fish stew is made. Going inland a little, the towns of Arles in Provence and Toulouse in Languedoc are noted for their sausage and charcuterie.

To the east of France are the **Alps** and the **Savoie province**. As would be expected from an alpine area, cheese and dairy produce are the local specialities. A good white wine is also produced and the charcuterie is also notable – in fact, any food that can see the people through the long snowy winters. It is in this region that Chartreuse is made.

Alsace and Lorraine are similar provinces and both have a strong German influence in their cuisine. Cheeses, pâté and other charcuterie, sauerkraut and the local wines are all reminiscent of Germany and quite unlike any other part of France. The local beer is famous, as are the locally made white brandies flavoured with wild fruit, raspberries, myrtle berries and – the most famous – cherries, known as Kirsch. The most well-known dishes are of course Quiche Lorraine and pâté de Foie gras from Strasbourg.

Coming inland on a broad front one comes to the two great wine growing regions of **Champagne and Burgundy**. These need no explanation. Dishes termed 'à la Bourguignonne' are essentially cooked in a Burgundy wine. The snails in this area are extremely good. Dijon in Burgundy is famous for its locally produced mustard.

The Midi of France is a vast area and each province boasts its own specialities. Wines are widely grown and local charcuterie is worth trying in practically every town. There are also many individual recipes for interesting stews using locally produced ingredients. The province of Périgord is famous for truffles, pâté de foie gras (which rivals that made in Strasbourg) and walnuts, from which a liqueur is made. Delicious edible fungi such as cèpes and chantrelle are found in this area. There is also an abundance of fish: carp, pike, crayfish and salmon from the many freshwater rivers and streams. To the north of the area, Orleans is known for vinegar 'à l'ancienne' which originated here, and the town of Pithiviers is known for a gâteau, sold locally, bearing the name of the town.

Basic ingredients

French cooking stands in a class of its own because French housewives take great trouble not only to use the best, freshest and most perfect ingredients but also to treat even the smallest ingredient with care and respect. At the beginning of the 18th century it was not unusual for a housewife to spend up to five or six hours preparing just one dish, but nowadays, economy and the pace of modern life has made it essential to cook the simpler dishes for everyday meals. It is still important to shop with great care, inspecting each purchase, especially of meat, fruit and vegetables. It is false economy to buy any food but the best, as you will never be able to cook a perfect French dish while the basic ingredients are inferior. Although it is not necessary to use expensive ingredients, use each one carefully, blending the flavours to produce a delicious dish.

The choice of fat and oil is important. Whether you choose to use butter, margarine, lard, dripping, olive oil or corn oil, use the best quality available. Many of the regional dishes traditionally call for goose, chicken or meat dripping. The flavour that butter imparts is unequalled for cakes, sauces and special dishes such as those 'au beurre' or 'à la meunière'. Margarine is sometimes preferred for health reasons and can be used instead of butter as it still gives a good colour and texture to your cooking. Oil is used frequently instead of fat for savoury dishes and frying. Corn oil and groundnut oil are the most economical

Wine used in cooking

and can be used for deep frying or added to butter (equal quantities) when sautéing ingredients. Using a mixture of butter and oil has the advantage of a good butter flavour without the butter becoming too brown. If a recipe calls for olive oil, do make sure that you use it. Although olive is more expensive than other cooking oils, nothing can rival it for flavour, especially in salad dressings or the classic vegetable stew, rataouille.

Onions, shallots and garlic are all important ingredients for French savoury dishes. When gently fried and browned, they caramellize, imparting a delicious flavour and the dish takes on a brown colour. Always cook them slowly; if they catch and burn the resulting flavour will be bitter. White sauces and meat dishes are often flavoured with onion softened but not browned. Sometimes this is achieved by cooking a whole bulb, studded with cloves, in with the stock, milk or cooking liquid, to be removed before the dish is served.

Good rich stock, whether beef, veal, chicken or fish, is an ingredient essential to French cooking. For a truly delicious soup or sauce, it is worth going to all the trouble of making stock. Rarely does one find a stock pot in anyone's kitchen nowadays, but many cooks make stock to store in the refrigerator and boil up every 3 or

4 days with any suitable scraps which may have been collected since the last boil-up. Alternatively, if you own a deep freezing unit, make your own stock and store it frozen in a concentrated form, the size of ice cubes. In an emergency, use a chicken or beef stock cube, but do not expect your cooking to retain its individual flavour.

Cheese, eggs and cream are widely used in French cooking. If a French cheese is specified in a recipe, try to use that one. Some cheeses are chosen for flavour, others for their melting properties and texture. Eggs should be as fresh as possible. Frequently the yolks only are used and these, in conjunction with cream, give a dish its smoothness and richness. They are used to thicken and add flavour to many savoury as well as sweet dishes. Egg whites can give a light and fluffy texture to a dish – as shown in a carefully prepared and well-risen soufflé.

Wine plays an extremely important part in French cooking. Use as good a quality wine as you can afford. There are very few 'rules' as to which colour of wine to use, as most meats can be cooked successfully in either. It is a good idea, however, to serve the same wine with the dish at table as that used for cooking. Wine should always be cooked for a long time to evaporate the alcohol and impart its unique flavour. Add it to stews, casseroles and to the roasting pan for roasting meat, at the beginning of the cooking time. If it is to be used in a dish which only has a short cooking time, put the wine in a small saucepan and boil it rapidly until reduced to about $\frac{1}{3}$ of the original quantity before using it.

Herbs are best when used fresh, not dried. Growing your own is quite simple, even if you have no garden. Try them in a window box – they smell superb. The most important herbs used in French cooking are those comprising a bouquet garni – a bay leaf, a sprig of thyme and some stalks of parsley. Basil, tarragon and chives are also widely used. It is useful to know that 1 tablespoon ($1\frac{1}{4}$T) fresh chopped herbs is equivalent to 1 teaspoon dried chopped herbs.

Vinegar is used quite widely in French cooking. The best sort to use is a good wine vinegar, white or red, according to taste or the recipe. Flavoured vinegars can be bought but you can make your own if you like: e.g. Tarragon vinegar can be made by adding a large sprig of fresh tarragon to the bottle of vinegar. Leave for at least 1 month before using.

Salt and pepper are essential for all cooking. The freshly ground variety, whether rock salt, or black or white peppercorns, have more flavour and are distinctly preferable to the already prepared powders.

Quiche Lorraine (1)
Tuna fish Provençale (2)
Pâtés (3)
A selection of French cheeses (4)
Lobster bisque (5)
Scallops Breton-style (6)
Cheese omelette (7)

5

6

7

Cooking utensils
(Batterie de Cuisine)

The French like to use the right tools for each job. This doesn't mean that they own a lot of gimmicky gadgets, but simple basic equipment which will perform each task quickly and with the least possible fuss. You probably possess the majority of utensils needed in your kitchen, but might like to buy just one or two of the more typically French moulds, terrines and tourtières, to complete your collection. The following utensils are those most common in French kitchens.

Pans. You would probably find a minimum of 12 pans in each kitchen. These cover every contingency from sauce-making to cooking whole fish. The following pans are a must – a set of 3 saucepans of varying size, with one large enough to hold a whole chicken.

Sauté pan	Steamer
Frying pan	Fish kettle
Deep frying pan	Preserving pan
Double saucepan	Roasting pan
(double boiler)	
Omelette pan	
(6 or 7 inch diameter)	

Copper is the best choice of metal as it is an excellent heat conductor and gives even heating over the base of the whole pan. Copper, however, can taint food and so each pan must be tin-lined. Stainless steel is a practical metal from the cleaning point of view, but a poor conductor of heat, so the base of the pans must be coated with copper. Cast iron and good quality enamelled aluminium pans are all acceptable.

Mixing bowls of all sizes are essential. It is impossible to advise on the number but the more you have, in as many different sizes, the easier life will be. If you are a really keen cook, you may like to possess the large spherical-style copper bowl which the French use only for whisking egg whites. Without a doubt you will get a better volume and a better texture to egg whites when they are whisked thus.

Knives are one of the most important elements of a good set of kitchen equipment. Always buy the best quality available and they will last for years. Steel knives can be kept sharper than stainless steel knives, although it is a good idea to have a mixture of both. Fruit discolours steel very badly and steel will rust quickly unless great care is taken.

A large French cook's knife (essential)

A vegetable knife (stainless steel)

A ham knife for cutting cold meat

A carving knife

A bread knife

A palette knife, best in stainless steel with a very flexible blade

Other useful cutting utensils are a **can opener**, a **potato peeler**, which can be used for paring fruit thinly or for removing the thin zest of citrus fruits and a mandolin for cutting wafer-thin slices of cucumber – or even cutting potatoes for game chips. **Kitchen scissors** are a must.

Large kitchen forks are useful – make sure you have at least one large carving fork.

Spoons: wooden spoons, large metal spoons for basting, slotted spoons and standard measuring spoons are a must. It is impossible to collect too many. **Wire whisks**, flat and balloon shaped, are also a help.

Three **strainers** are useful: a hair or nylon sieve in a wooden frame for puréeing fruit and vegetables, a conical 'chinois' strainer for soups and sauces, a bowl sieve for sifting dry ingredients.

A colander is a must for draining vegetables.

A cheese grater and a **nutmeg grater** are essential.

A good quality teak **chopping board** is a good investment as it will last for years and save your work surfaces. A pastry board is not now considered important as pastry can be rolled out on plastic work surfaces. The rolling pin is still a must. A marble slab is useful for making pastry the French way to keep it as cool as possible.

Weighing scales are essential, if you are a really serious cook, for accurate measuring.

A set of measuring jugs is convenient to use for measuring liquid ingredients.

Ovenproof and flameproof casseroles are available varying from very modern designs to the classic earthenware. The term 'casserole' in France denotes a wide variety of cooking utensils from saucepans to cocottes and ramekins.

A terrine is an earthenware oblong or oval dish, with a lid, which is classically used for cooking pâtés.

Many different **moulds** are used in French cooking for both sweet and savoury dishes. Some of the most common are:

Moule à manqué (a shallow cake tin with sloping sides)

Moule à charlotte (a deep oval or round mould with sloping sides)

Moule à dariole (a small round mould with tall sloping sides. Used for individual servings)

Moule à douille (this is the collective name for the many varieties of ring moulds used in French cooking)

Moule à pâté (hinged mould for raised pies)

Moule à gelée (decorative jelly mould)

Moules à madeleines (shell-shaped moulds for cooking madelines)

Timbale is yet another kind of a mould, usually round with straight or slightly sloping sides. It can be large or for individual portions and the food dish frequently includes timbale in its name e.g. Timbale de Champignon. A soufflé dish is a Timbale à soufflé.

Tart tins, (tourtières) are another must. They can be metal with a removeable base or ovenproof china. Tarts can also be made in a fluted flan ring standing on a baking tray. Savoury flans are made in a plain flan ring. Two or three baking trays are essential in every kitchen.

A loaf tin and a selection of deep and shallow cake and patty tins are useful. Biscuit cutters, both plain and fluted, and icing pipes and a bag, are desirable.

A food mixer with a blender attachment will certainly save you time.

There are many other pieces of equipment which, although not really essential, are decorative in the kitchen: a pestle and mortar for crushing spices, an hachinette for chopping herbs, a garlic press, a salt and pepper mill, au gratin dishes, a larding needle, a meat mallet and so on.

Genoise sponge in preparation

Without its famous sauces, French cuisine would be sadly lacking. It is these all-important and delicately flavoured sauces which are the basis of most of the particularly delicious dishes. French housewives know the value of taking a little extra care with the preparation and flavouring so that their sauces emerge as the final crowning glory to their cooking.

The roux sauces, such as Espagnole sauce and béchamel sauce take their flavour from the careful blending of ingredients at the beginning and then the cooking of the butter and flour roux to ensure that the sauce is neither greasy nor floury tasting. If the roux is properly cooked, it is possible to add the liquid all at once, not gradually, and still have a smooth sauce. I find that it is easier to blend a sauce if I use a wire whisk instead of a wooden spoon when adding the liquid. If you have to keep the sauce hot before serving, try pouring on a small amount of milk to cover the top of the sauce. Beat the milk in just before serving.

Sauces

Butter sauces take their flavour from the eggs and butter used in making them. They have an extremely delicate flavour which makes them generally of more use in haute cuisine than when cooking for the family. These sauces are generally served warm rather than hot.

Home made mayonnaise is superb and far preferable to the commercial variety. Before you start, make sure that all your utensils are clean, free from grease and well dried. The oil must be added very slowly at first or the mayonnaise may curdle. If this does happen, place another egg yolk in a clean bowl and add the curdled mixture to this, drop by drop, beating well all the time. Mayonnaise can be kept for a short while at room temperature – do not put it in the refrigerator as it will tend to separate.

Sweet sauces are not made as frequently as the savoury variety but they are well worth the trouble for a special dinner party. Nothing can rival the flavour of a freshly made fruit sauce or chocolate sauce.

Salmon trout in aspic (left)

Veal loaf coated in sauce chaudfroid and a layer of aspic (below)

Meat served with a white sauce (bottom)

Sauce espagnole   Rich brown sauce

2 oz. (4T) butter or dripping
2 oz. (½ cup) diced bacon
½ onion, sliced
½ carrot, sliced
1 shallot, chopped
2 oz. (½ cup) plain (all purpose) flour
1 pint (2½ cups) fond brun (beef bone stock, see recipe page 30)
6 mushroom stalks
2 tablespoons tomato paste
2 tablespoons dry sherry
salt and pepper

Melt the butter or dripping in a small heavy saucepan. Add the bacon and fry until softened. Add the prepared vegetables and continue frying until they are softened but not browned. Stir in the flour and cook very gently, stirring occasionally, until the whole is a rich, russet brown (this will probably take about 20–30 minutes). Add stock and mushroom stalks. Bring to the boil, stirring, simmer for 30 minutes. Add tomato paste, sherry and seasonings, simmer for a further 15 minutes. Strain the sauce, pressing the vegetables well to extract as much liquid as possible.
Reheat. Use as required.

Sauce madère   Madeira sauce

½ pint (1¼ cups) sauce espagnole
3 tablespoons (¼ cup) Madeira wine

Serve with meat and game.

Prepare the sauce espagnole, stir in Madeira wine. Reheat without boiling. Use as required.

Sauce chasseur

1 tablespoon (1¼T) oil
1 oz. (2T) butter
4 shallots, chopped
4 oz. mushrooms, finely sliced
¼ pint (⅝ cup) white wine
½ pint (1¼ cups) sauce espagnole
extra 1 oz. butter
pinch of chopped parsley
pinch of chopped tarragon

Serve with chicken, rabbit and other meats.

Heat the oil and butter in a small saucepan. Add the shallots and mushrooms and fry until the mushrooms are cooked. Pour in the wine, bring to the boil and boil until the wine is reduced by half. Stir in the sauce espagnole, butter and herbs. Simmer 2–3 minutes. Use as required.

Sauce robert

1 small onion, chopped
½ oz. (1T) butter
¼ pint (⅝ cup) vinegar
½ pint (⅝ cup) sauce espagnole
2 gherkins, chopped
2 teaspoons French mustard
1 teaspoon chopped parsley

Serve with pork, lamb, liver and kidneys.

Place the onion in a small saucepan with butter. Fry gently until softened, add the vinegar, boil until reduced by half. Add the sauce espagnole, bring to the boil and simmer for 15 minutes. Add the gherkins, mustard and parsley just before serving. Do not re-boil.

Sauce béchamel   White sauce

1 shallot
1 carrot
1 stick celery
1 small bayleaf
10 white peppercorns
1 blade mace
1 pint (2½ cups) milk
2 oz. (4T) butter
2 oz. (½ cup) plain (all purpose) flour
salt

Peel and slice the shallot and carrot. Chop the celery. Place the vegetables in a saucepan with the bayleaf, peppercorns, mace and milk. Heat gently until boiling. Cover the pan and leave for 15–20 minutes. Strain the milk, discard the vegetables and spices. Melt the butter in a clean saucepan, stir in the flour and cook over a low heat until the flour is cooked but not browned (it will have a 'honeycomb' appearance), for about 2–4 minutes. Add the milk, stirring continuously, bring to the boil and simmer 5–7 minutes. Add salt to taste. Use as required.

Sauce mornay added to eggs Florentine

Sauce soubise — Onion sauce

½ pint (1¼ cups) sauce béchamel
3 onions
¼ pint (⅝ cup) fond blanc de
volaille (chicken stock) (see
recipe page 30)
salt and pepper
pinch of sugar

Serve with eggs, vegetables, fish or lamb.

Prepare the sauce béchamel.
Peel the onions and slice. Place in a saucepan with the stock, bring
to the boil and simmer until the onions are very tender. Drain the
onions and either chop finely or purée in an electric blender. Mix the
onion with the sauce béchamel, adjust seasoning, add sugar. Reheat
and serve as required.

Sauce aurore — Tomato cream sauce

½ pint (1¼ cups) sauce béchamel
½ pint (1¼ cups) tomato purée
or sauce tomate (see page 20)
sugar
salt and pepper

Serve with fish, meat, eggs and vegetables.

Heat the sauce béchamel in a small saucepan until boiling. Add the
tomato purée or sauce and bring to the boil, stirring constantly.
Simmer for 3–5 minutes. Strain the sauce, reheat in a clean saucepan
and adjust seasoning as necessary with sugar, salt and pepper. If the
sauce is too thin, bring to the boil and continue boiling until it
reaches the desired consistency. Use as required.

Sauce mornay — Cheese sauce

½ pint (1¼ cups) sauce béchamel
1 oz. (¼ cup) grated
Cheddar cheese
1 oz. (¼ cup) grated
Parmesan cheese
salt, pepper and mustard

Serve with eggs, vegetables, fish and pasta.

Heat the sauce béchamel in a small saucepan, stirring, until it boils.
Remove from heat, whisk in the grated cheeses. Reheat, without
boiling, whisking until the cheese is melted. Add salt, pepper and
mustard to taste. Use as required.

Sauce béarnaise

3 tablespoons (1¼ cup) white
wine vinegar
6 peppercorns
1 shallot, chopped
¼ pint (⅝ cup) sauce béchamel
2 egg yolks
1 oz. (2T) butter
salt and pepper

Serve with vegetables, fish and grilled meat.

Place the vinegar, peppercorns and shallot in a small saucepan. Bring to the boil and boil until the vinegar is reduced to 1 tablespoon. Strain. Put the sauce béchamel in a bowl, add the reduced vinegar and the egg yolks. Place the bowl over a saucepan of simmering water (do not allow the bowl to touch the water). Stir continuously with a wooden spoon.
Add the butter in small pieces, heating continuously. Do not overheat the sauce or it will curdle. If this happens, add 1 tablespoon of very cold water and beat well again. When sauce is the consistency of thick mayonnaise, season to taste.
Use as required.

note: a different flavour can be achieved if 2 tablespoons wine vinegar and 1 tablespoon tarragon vinegar are used. A few drops of chilli vinegar can also be added.

Timbale de champignon

Savoury egg custard with mushroom sauce

3 eggs
¾ pint (approx. 2 cups) milk
3 oz. (¾ cup) grated
Cheddar cheese
salt and pepper
¼ teaspoon dry mustard
½ pint (1¼ cups) sauce béchamel
(see recipe page 16)
4 oz. (1 cup) button mushrooms

A timbale is a type of mould. The word timbale in a recipe title generally means that the dish is cooked in a timbale and served unmoulded.

Beat the eggs lightly, add the warmed milk and cheese and stir to mix. Season to taste with salt, pepper and mustard. Pour egg mixture into a small soufflé dish or charlotte mould. Stand mould in a roasting pan, add water to about 1 inch depth. Bake in a moderately slow oven (325°F. Mark 3) for 50 minutes or until set.
Prepare the béchamel sauce. Slice the mushrooms finely, stir them into the sauce and cook for a further 2–3 minutes.
Turn the timbale out of the mould on to a heated serving dish, pour the sauce over the top and serve immediately.

note: this can also be made in individual dariole moulds. Reduce the cooking time to about 25 minutes.

serves 4

Sauce choron

1 quantity sauce béarnaise
1 tablespoon tomato paste

Serve with fish, particularly salmon.

Prepare the sauce béarnaise.
Whisk in the tomato paste just before the sauce is completed. Use as required.

Sauce valois

1 quantity sauce béarnaise
1 tablespoon (1¼T) tomato paste

Serve with chicken or veal.

Prepare sauce béarnaise.
Add the warmed beef extract just before the sauce is completed. Use as required.

Sauce velouté

1 oz. (2T) butter
6 white peppercorns
3 parsley stalks
1 oz. (¼ cup) plain (all purpose) flour
¾ pint (approx. 2 cups) fond blanc or fond blanc de volaille (white stock or chicken stock, see recipes page 30)
4 mushroom stalks
juice of ¼ lemon
salt
1 tablespoon (1¼T) single (light) cream

Melt the butter in a small saucepan. Add the peppercorns, parsley stalks and flour. Cook gently, stirring continuously, until the flour is cooked but not browned (it will have a 'honeycomb' appearance) about 2–4 minutes. Add the stock, stirring, and bring to the boil. Add the mushroom stalks, lemon juice and salt to taste. Simmer gently for 20–25 minutes, stirring occasionally. Strain the sauce, add the cream and reheat without boiling. Use as required.

Sauce hollandaise

juice of ½ a lemon
1 teaspoon water
2 egg yolks
4 oz. (8T) butter
salt and cayenne pepper

Serve with vegetables, fish and eggs.

Place the lemon juice and water in a small bowl. Put the bowl over a saucepan of simmering water (do not let it touch the water). Add the egg yolks and ½ oz. butter. Whisk very thoroughly until stiff enough to retain the marks of the whisk.
Remove the saucepan from the heat and add the remaining butter in very small pieces, whisking well all the time.
Season to taste with salt and cayenne pepper.
Use as required.

Sauce verte
Green sauce

1 quantity sauce hollandaise
4 oz. (½ cup) finely chopped
cooked spinach
salt and pepper

Serve with seafood.

As soon as the sauce hollandaise is cooked, whisk in the spinach, off the heat. When thoroughly combined, reheat very carefully without boiling. Adjust the seasoning. Use as required.

Sauce bercy

½ oz. (1T) butter
2 shallots, chopped
¼ pint (⅝ cup) white wine
1 pint (2½ cups) fond blanc,
fond blanc de volaille or fond de
poisson (white stock, chicken
stock or fish stock, see recipes
page 30)
salt and pepper
juice of ½ lemon
1 tablespoon (1¼T)
chopped parsley
extra ¾ oz. (scant ⅛ cup)
butter, softened
¾ oz. (scant ¼ cup) plain (all
purpose) flour

Serve, according to the stock used, with eggs, veal, vegetables and fish.

Melt the butter in a saucepan, add the shallots and cook gently until softened but not browned. Add the wine and boil. Cook until the wine is reduced by half.
Add the stock, seasoning, lemon juice and parsley. Bring to the boil, then remove from the heat.
Cream the extra butter and flour together well. Add to the saucepan in very small pieces, stirring until well blended. Bring to the boil, simmer 1–2 minutes.
Use as required.

Sauce de tomates provençale
Tomato sauce Provençale-style

2 lb. tomatoes
2 tablespoons (2½T) olive oil
1 clove garlic, crushed
1 bayleaf
1 small onion finely chopped
1 small carrot, finely chopped
1 stick celery, finely chopped
bouquet garni
salt, pepper and sugar

Serve with meat or fish.

Skin the tomatoes, remove the seeds and chop roughly.
Heat the oil in a saucepan, add the tomatoes, garlic, bayleaf, vegetables and bouquet garni. Cover the pan tightly and simmer for 30 minutes.
Remove the bouquet garni and bayleaf. Season with salt, pepper and sugar to taste. Sieve the sauce or purée in an electric blender if a smooth sauce is desired. Use as required.

Mayonnaise

2 egg yolks
2 tablespoons (2½T)
tarragon vinegar
¼ teaspoon each salt, pepper and
mustard
pinch of sugar
½–¾ pint (1¼-approx. 2 cups)
olive oil

Place the egg yolks, vinegar, salt, pepper, mustard and sugar in a clean bowl. Whisk with a fork or beat with a wooden spoon until creamy.
Add the oil, drop by drop, beating well all the time. When half the oil has been added, add the remainder in a slow but steady stream. Beat until a smooth thick sauce is formed. If it becomes too thick, add a little boiling water.

note: mayonnaise will keep, if stored in a clean screw-top jar, for about 1 month.

Sauce tartare

½ pint (1¼ cups) mayonnaise
1 teaspoon chopped capers
1 teaspoon chopped gherkins
1 teaspoon chopped mixed herbs
1 hard-boiled egg white, chopped
salt and pepper

Serve with grilled or fried fish.

Combine all the ingredients together. Season to taste. Use as required.

Sauce aïoli   Garlic sauce

Serve with cold meats, fish and shellfish.

Make the mayonnaise as described above, using a scant ½ pint (1¼ cups) olive oil. Add 3–4 well crushed cloves of garlic to the egg yolks before adding the oil.

Sauce vinaigrette   Vinaigrette dressing

¼ teaspoon each, salt, pepper and dry mustard
3 tablespoons (3¾T) olive oil
1 tablespoon (1¼T) vinegar

Serve with salads and cooked meats.

Place the seasonings in a bowl, add a little oil and mix to a smooth paste, add the remaining oil and then the vinegar. Whisk very briskly until the sauce is emulsified and the vinegar and oil thoroughly mixed.
Use as required.

note: add 1 clove garlic, crushed, 1 teaspoon mixed chopped dried herbs and 1 small onion, finely chopped, for a more flavoursome dressing.

Aspic

2 pints (5 cups) well flavoured stock (beef, veal or fish, according to the dish to be decorated)
¼ pint (⅝ cup) sherry
1 tablespoon (1¼T) vinegar
2 oz. (6 tablespoons) gelatine
2 egg whites

Aspic jelly (jello) plays a big part in French cold cookery. It can be used for setting savoury ingredients in a mould or for giving the dish a glazed appearance. It is nearly always used to line a mould before the savoury mousse or cream is put in to set. Alternatively, half-set aspic jelly (jello) is spooned over the dish.
It is possible to buy commercially prepared aspic jelly (jello) crystals but for a special occasion you may feel it would be worthwhile making your own.

Place the cold stock, sherry, vinegar and gelatine in a large saucepan. Heat slowly over a gentle heat, stirring occasionally. Whisk the egg whites until frothy, add them to the saucepan and whisk, over a low heat, until boiling. Allow the mixture to boil to the top of the pan without whisking, draw the pan aside. Repeat the boiling and drawing aside process twice more. Put aside for 5 minutes.
Strain the mixture through a scalded jelly (jello) bag or several thicknesses of muslin.
Use as required.

Sauce chaudfroid

¾ pint (approx. 2 cups) sauce béchamel (see recipe page 16) (make this sauce using 1 oz. (2T) butter, 1 oz. plain (all purpose) flour, ¾ pint milk)
2 tablespoons (2½T) aspic, made double strength
2 tablespoons (2½T) single (light) cream
salt and pepper

For coating cold fish, eggs and chicken.

Combine all the ingredients together thoroughly. Cool, stirring frequently to keep the sauce smooth.
When set to the consistency of thick cream, use for coating the cold foods.

note: for Chaudfroid brown sauce, use sauce espagnole (see recipe page 16) instead of sauce béchamel. Use for coating cold game, duck, cutlets and so on.

Sauce au chocolat Chocolate sauce

2 oz. plain dark chocolate
2 tablespoons (2½T) water
1 teaspoon cornflour
(cornstarch)
¼ pint (⅝ cup) milk
1 teaspoon castor
(superfine) sugar
½ teaspoon vanilla essence
1 tablespoon (1¼T) single (light)
cream, optional

Grate the chocolate into a saucepan, add the water and heat gently, without boiling, until chocolate has melted and combined with the water.
Mix the cornflour with the milk, add to saucepan. Bring to the boil, stirring constantly, simmer 4–5 minutes.
Add the sugar and vanilla essence and stir until the sugar is dissolved. Stir in the cream when the sauce has cooled slightly, do not reboil.
note: for a thicker sauce, halve the amount of milk used.

Sauce d'abricots Apricot sauce

3 tablespoons (¼ cup)
apricot jam
8 fl. oz. (1 cup) water
½ tablespoon arrowroot
lemon juice and sugar to taste

Place the apricot jam and water in a saucepan. Bring to the boil, stirring constantly. Mix the arrowroot with a very little extra water, add to the saucepan, bring to the boil and cook until clear, stirring constantly.
Add the sugar and lemon juice to taste. Sieve the sauce.
Use as required.

Sauce aux fruits Fruit sauce

Fruit purée
sugar
arrowroot

Place the fruit purée in a saucepan. Bring to the boil, add sugar to taste and stir until the sugar is dissolved. If the purée is very thin, thicken with 1 teaspoon arrowroot for every ½ pint (1¼ cups) purée. Mix the arrowroot with a little fruit juice or water before adding it to the pan. Bring to the boil and stir until the sauce clears. Serve as soon as possible.

Choux buns with fruit sauce

Pears with ice cream and chocolate sauce

note: the following fruits are most suitable for this sauce: currants, stoned (pitted) fruits, apples, berries.

Ham mousse

Hors d'oeuvres

'Hors d'oeuvres' is the French for appetizers. This means all the light delicious dishes which can precede the main course of a luncheon or dinner party. Sometimes hors d'oeuvres can be served as well as a soup although this does not always follow. The hors d'oeuvres is served before a soup course.

An hors d'oeuvres should never be served in large portions. It is merely a small daintily prepared dish to tempt your guests towards what is to come. Choose the dish carefully so that it will not clash with the other courses on the menu. Avoid serving more than one fish dish, or more than one course featuring the same meat or vegetable. Select the hors d'oeuvres to complement the menu in colour, texture and taste.

Some hors d'oeuvres can be served as a light luncheon on their own. Other chapters in the book include recipes which (if made in smaller quantities) could be served as hors d'oeuvres.

Hors d'oeuvres variés Mixed hors d'oeuvres

Hors d'oeuvres variés should be a selection of daintily prepared cold dishes of meat, fish, egg, fruit and vegetables. Serve at least four together, making sure that each complements the other in colour, flavour and texture. A suitable choice might be: rice salad, sardines, tomato, egg, radish; or sliced Continental sausage, orange sections, potato salad, cucumber. All the dishes must be carefully prepared and the food served in iced water, vinegar, a vinaigrette dressing or home made mayonnaise (see recipes pages 21 and 20), as appropriate to prevent it becoming dry. Guests help themselves to a little of each dish.

Tomato Skin and slice tomatoes thinly. Arrange them in a dish, sprinkle with vinaigrette dressing and a little finely chopped parsley.

Cucumber Score the skin at intervals with the prongs of a fork. Slice thinly, arrange in a dish and cover with vinaigrette dressing or vinegar. Decorate with thin slices of radish.

Celeriac Cut washed celeriac into julienne strips. Add enough home made mayonnaise to moisten. Serve.

Beetroot Peel and slice beetroot thinly. If you have some aspic cutters, cut the slices in fancy shapes. Arrange in a serving dish, sprinkle with vinaigrette dressing. Garnish with snipped chives.

Radish Slice washed and trimmed radishes very thinly. Arrange in a dish, cover with iced water. Garnish with fine cress.

Potato Dice cooked potato and mix it with enough home made mayonnaise to moisten. Serve garnished with chopped parsley or snipped chives.

Rice Mix hot cooked rice with enough vinaigrette dressing to moisten. Leave to cool. Add a little finely chopped red and green capsicum. Toss and serve.

Macedoine of Vegetable Mix diced cooked vegetables together gently (carrot, parsnip, celery, sweetcorn, peas, for example). Add enough home made mayonnaise to moisten. Serve garnished with finely chopped parsley.

Pineapple Cut pineapple in neat dice, chill. Serve topped with chopped mint.

Orange Peel orange, remove all the pith. Either slice thinly or cut into segments. Arrange in a dish, sprinkle with vinaigrette dressing and garnish with chopped mint. (This dish is extra delicious with a few halves of peeled and stoned grapes added.)

Cold Sausage (Charcuterie) Remove skin if necessary and slice thinly. Arrange in a serving dish and either sprinkle with vinaigrette dressing or coat in home made mayonnaise.

Ham Dice cooked ham, add enough home made mayonnaise to moisten. Serve garnished with chopped parsley or a sprinkling of cayenne pepper.

Sardines Arrange whole drained sardines in a dish. Sprinkle with vinaigrette dressing. Garnish with finely chopped parsley and cayenne pepper in lines.

Egg Hard boil an egg, allow to become cold. Slice in thin rounds. Arrange slices in a dish on a bed of shredded lettuce. Coat with home made mayonnaise and serve garnished with a sprinkling of cayenne pepper.

Shrimps or Prawns Peel shrimps or prawns, add enough home made mayonnaise to moisten. Serve on a bed of shredded lettuce garnished with fine cress and some of the heads.

Asperge à la hollandaise
Asparagus with hollandaise sauce

4 bundles asparagus (about 10 stalks in each)
sauce hollandaise (see recipe page 19)

Trim the asparagus, remove any hard woody stem and clean well in cold water. Cook in boiling salted water to cover for 15–20 minutes or until just tender. Drain. Remove the string tying the bundles. Serve each bundle of asparagus on a heated serving plate with a spoonful of sauce hollandaise at one end. It is possible to buy special asparagus dishes on which to serve asparagus, with a separate place for the sauce.

note: each asparagus stalk is picked up individually with the fingertips, dipped in the sauce and then eaten. Supply finger bowls of iced water.

variation: an equally delicious but simpler way of serving asparagus is to serve it with melted butter instead of sauce hollandaise.

serves 4

Avocat vinaigrette
Avocado pear with vinaigrette dressing

2 ripe avocado pears
4 tablespoons (good ¼ cup) sauce vinaigrette (see recipe page 21)
lettuce for serving

Cut the avocado pears in half lengthways. Remove the stones carefully. Spoon a little sauce over the cut surfaces to prevent them from discolouring.
Place each half of avocado pear on a bed of lettuce on individual serving dishes. Spoon the remaining sauce vinaigrette into the hollows left by the stone.
Serve chilled.

variation: mix the sauce vinaigrette with 8 oz. (2 cups) peeled prawns (shrimp) and fill into the avocado pear halves.

serves 4

Salade de melon et jambon
Melon and ham salad

1 small honeydew melon
4 slices Bayonne ham
lettuce
8 black olives

Remove the melon flesh from the skin with a parisienne (melon-ball) cutter and cut into dice. Roll the ham up and secure each roll with a cocktail stick.
Place a bed of lettuce in each of 4 individual serving dishes or on plates. Put the melon on the lettuce and top with the ham. Garnish each dish with 2 black olives.
Serve chilled.

note: bayonne ham is a raw smoked ham prepared in the South West of France. If it is not available, use parma, prosciutto or westphalia ham as they are very similar.

serves 4

Pamplemousse au gingembre
Grapefruit with ginger

2 large grapefruit
sherry
¼ teaspoon each ground ginger and ground nutmeg
1 tablespoon (1¼T) finely chopped preserved ginger (in syrup)
2 glacé cherries
serves 4

Peel the grapefruit and remove all the pith. Cut them into segments, carefully removing all the skin.
Arrange the segments in individual serving glasses. Sprinkle with sherry, ground ginger and ground nutmeg, mixed together. Decorate each glass with chopped ginger and half a glacé (candied) cherry. Serve chilled. Serve sugar separately, if necessary.

Tomates farcies aux crevettes
Tomatoes stuffed with shrimps

4 large firm tomatoes
6 oz. (1½ cups) peeled shrimps
½ teaspoon dried basil
¼ pint (1¼ cups) home made mayonnaise (see recipe page 20)
lettuce for serving

serves 4

Skin the tomatoes and stand them firmly, stalk end underneath. Cut off the tops, scoop out the pulp and pips carefully with a teaspoon. Combine shrimps and basil with the home made mayonnaise, then spoon into the tomato cases.
Place a bed of lettuce on 4 individual serving plates and top with the stuffed tomatoes.

note: skin the tomatoes by plunging them in boiling water for 1 minute. Place in cold water until cool enough to handle, then peel skin off with a knife.

Salade de tomates
Tomato salad

6 firm red tomatoes
3 tablespoons (¼ cup) sauce vinaigrette (see recipe page 21)
1 teaspoon chopped capers
1 teaspoon finely chopped gherkin
1 teaspoon finely chopped parsley
serves 4

Tomato salad is a very popular appetizer for a meal in France, especially around the Mediterranean where the tomatoes are large and luscious.

Skin the tomatoes and slice thinly. Arrange the slices in a serving dish.
Mix the sauce vinaigrette with the capers, gherkin and parsley. Pour over the tomatoes. Serve.

Escargots au beurre
Snails in butter

4 dozen snails
3 cloves garlic
3 oz. (6T) butter
3 tablespoons (¼ cup) chopped parsley
2 tablespoons (scant ¼ cup) fine white breadcrumbs
freshly ground black pepper

serves 4

Wash the snails, place them in a large saucepan and cover with cold water. Bring to the boil, simmer 15–20 minutes. Remove the snails from their shell, rinse shells and put back the snails. Crush the cloves of garlic, then add the butter, parsley, breadcrumbs and black pepper. Beat until smooth.
Place a little butter mixture into each shell on top of the snails.
Place snails on a heatproof dish and place in a very hot oven (450°F. Mark 8) until the butter is sizzling.
Serve immediately in the shells.

note: snails must be fasted for a week before cooking if they are gathered fresh. They have sometimes eaten things which would be poisonous to man. The day before cooking, wash them well and cover with salted water until needed.

Grenouilles à la Lyonnaise
Frog's legs lyonnaise

2×3⅔ oz. cans or 8 oz. fresh frogs legs
flour
salt and pepper
1 onion
2 oz. (4T) butter
1 teaspoon wine vinegar
chopped parsley for garnish

serves 4

Although frog's legs are not always considered such a delicacy outside France, they are nevertheless an ideal way to start a typical French meal. They can be cooked in a very wide variety of ways but the following recipe is particularly delicious.

Drain canned frog's legs. If fresh frog's legs are used, remove feet, skin them and skewer; soak in iced water for 6–8 hours, changing the water every 2 hours.
Season the flour with salt and pepper. Coat the frog's legs in flour. Slice the onion very thinly.
Melt the butter in a frying pan, add the onion rings and fry them until softened. Add the frog's legs to the pan and continue cooking for 2–3 minutes.
Place the onion and the frog's legs in a heated serving dish. Add the vinegar to the butter in pan and reheat. Sprinkle the frog's legs with parsley, pour the butter over and serve immediately.

Spooning half-set aspic over veal galantine

Galantine de veau   Veal loaf

8 oz. minced lean veal
4 oz. pork sausage meat
4 oz. streaky bacon, chopped
3 oz. (1 cup) soft white breadcrumbs
salt and pepper
¼ teaspoon ground nutmeg
½ teaspoon dried mixed herbs
1 egg
2 tablespoons water
3 hard-boiled eggs, shelled
sauce chaudfroid (see recipe page 21)
extra aspic jelly (jello)
cucumber and radish for garnish

Mix together thoroughly the veal, sausage meat, bacon, breadcrumbs, salt and pepper, nutmeg, herbs, egg and water. Scald a pudding cloth by pouring boiling water through it. Spread the meat mixture on to the cloth and lay the eggs in the centre. Form into a short thick roll. Tie pudding cloth firmly. Cook in boiling water, to cover, for 2–2½ hours.
Press under a heavy weight until cold. Place on a cake rack and spoon the sauce chaudfroid over. When the sauce is set, cover with a layer of aspic. Garnish with thin rounds of cucumber and radish, dipped in aspic jelly (jello).

note: Veal Galantine can be made in a terrine or loaf tin. Cook as for Terrine de campagne (*overleaf*). The sauce chaudfroid and aspic may be omitted.

Blanchaille au naturel   Fried whitebait

1 lb. whitebait
flour
salt
pepper
oil or fat for deep frying
lemon wedges and thin slices of brown bread and butter for serving

Whitebait are too small to be drawn, so make sure that they are as fresh as possible. They are a considered delicacy on the French coast—where they are prepared as soon as the day's catch of fish is sold. Do not wash them unless absolutely necessary and handle them as little as possible.

Remove weed and any grit from the whitebait. Mix the flour with salt and pepper and dredge the whitebait with it
Heat the oil until 375°F. (a ¼ inch dice of bread will brown in less than a minute) or fat until a faint blue haze rises from the surface. Place a handful of whitebait in the frying basket and fry for 2 minutes. Drain on absorbent kitchen paper. Continue until all the whitebait has been fried.
Just before serving, reheat oil or fat and refry all the whitebait together for 1–2 minutes or until crisp but not dry. Drain on absorbent kitchen paper.
Serve on individual heated serving plates sprinkled with extra salt and pepper. Garnish with lemon wedges. Serve the brown bread and

serves 4   butter separately.

Mousse au jambon · Ham mousse

8 oz. ham
1 teaspoon tomato paste
¾ oz. (2¼ tablespoons) gelatine
¼ pint (⅝ cup) fond blanc (white stock, see recipe page 30)
¼ pint (⅝ cup) sauce béchamel (see recipe page 16)
salt and pepper
¼ pint (⅝ cup) double heavy cream
2 egg whites
serves 4

Mince the ham twice and beat very thoroughly with the tomato paste. Press through a wire sieve or cream in an electric blender. Dissolve the gelatine in the heated stock and allow to cool. Beat the béchamel sauce into the ham mixture with the stock and gelatine, season. Allow to cool until beginning to set. Half whip the cream. Whisk the egg whites until stiff. Fold the cream and egg whites into the ham mixture.
Spoon into individual serving dishes or a prepared soufflé case (see page 43).
Put in a cool place until set. Garnish as desired.

Pâté normand · Pâté Normandy-style

8 oz. minced pork
8 oz. minced veal
4 oz. minced pigs tongue
4 oz. minced pigs liver
4 oz. minced bacon
2 oz. minced pork fat
3 cloves garlic, crushed
¼ teaspoon each ground nutmeg, ground cloves, dried thyme, dried basil
½ teaspoon salt
¼ teaspoon freshly ground black pepper
¼ pint (⅝ cup) dry sherry
8 rashers streaky bacon

Mix all the ingredients, except the rashers of streaky bacon, thoroughly. Line a terrine with 6 of the bacon rashers, fill with the meat mixture and press down very firmly. Cover with the remaining bacon rashers. Cover the pâté with aluminium foil and cook in a moderate oven (350°F. Mark 4) for 1½ hours.
Cool. Place cooked pâté in a cool place or in the refrigerator for 6–8 hours before turning out and cutting.

note: the meats may have to be minced 2–3 times to get the necessary smoothness.

Rillettes de Porc · Potted pork

1 lb. belly pork
8 oz. pork fat
1 clove garlic, crushed
1 teaspoon chopped mixed herbs
½ teaspoon salt
¼ teaspoon freshly ground black pepper
3 tablespoons (¼ cup) water

Chop the meat into short thin strips. Dice the pork fat. Mix with all the remaining ingredients and pile into an earthenware or enamelled dish. Cover with aluminium foil.
Bake rillettes in a very slow oven (275°F. Mark 1) for 3–4 hours.
The pork should be very soft and swimming in its own fat. Adjust the seasoning.
Drain off all the fat. Mash rillettes thoroughly with a fork. Pack into small earthenware pots, covering with the fat. Cover with aluminium foil and store in the refrigerator.

Terrine de campagne · Terrine country-style

8 oz. fat belly pork, minced
4 oz. minced lean veal
8 oz. minced chicken livers
2 tablespoons (scant ¼ cup) dry white wine
2 tablespoons (scant ¼ cup) brandy
1 oz. pork fat, diced
3 black peppercorns
3 juniper berries
1 clove garlic, crushed
¼ teaspoon ground mace
½ teaspoon salt
8 rashers streaky bacon

A terrine is the mould in which a pâté is sometimes cooked. Hence the word terrine in a recipe title indicates that it is a pâté cooked in a terrine.

Mix all the ingredients (except the bacon rashers) together very thoroughly.
Line a terrine with 6 rashers of the bacon. Fill with the meat mixture, press down well. Top with the remaining bacon rashers. Stand terrine in a roasting pan with water 1 inch deep. Cook in a slow oven (300°F. Mark 2) for 1½ hours or until the meat starts to shrink away from the edge.
Cool, press with a heavy weight and store in the refrigerator. Seal with melted pork fat if the terrine is to be kept for more than a week.

Soups

There are too many French soups to be able to mention them all but certainly the French can claim some of the most delicious in the world. Every French housewife knows the value of having some good stock always on hand. She is then ready to produce, almost at a moment's notice, practically any soup you can mention with its own individual home made flavour. (See introduction).

Soup is served with nearly every meal in France. Whether it is the lightest lunch or the most elaborate dinner party, there is a suitable soup for the occasion: a substantial garbure for a winter supper or a vichyssoise for a smaller luncheon, consommé en gelée for a summer dinner party or potage à la hollandaise for a formal winter dinner – the suggestions are almost endless.

A tureen is the best container in which to serve soup as it can sit decoratively on the table and you can serve second helpings if required. It is a good idea to have two types of soup dishes, one for the family soups, with a wide top, and small bouillon cups for lighter, more delicate soups.

Fond brun　Beef bone stock

2 lb. beef bones
1 onion
1 carrot
1 turnip
1 leek
4 pints (10 cups) water
½ teaspoon salt
4 peppercorns
½ teaspoon meat extract

Wash the bones and trim off excess fat. Prepare the vegetables and chop them into large pieces. Place all the ingredients in a large saucepan.
Bring the stock to the boil, cover and simmer slowly for 4–5 hours. Skim frequently.
Strain the stock. Either allow it to become cold and remove the fat or lay strips of absorbent kitchen paper across the surface of the hot stock to remove excess fat.
Use as required.

note: for a richer stock, add 4 oz. shin of beef, minced or finely chopped.

Fond blanc　White or veal stock

2 lb. veal bones
4 oz. veal, chopped
½ teaspoon salt
4 white peppercorns
4 pints (10 cups) cold water
1 onion
1 stick celery
1 carrot

Wash the bones, remove excess fat. Place the bones, meat, salt, peppercorns and water in a large saucepan. Bring to the boil slowly, skim.
Prepare the vegetables and chop roughly. Add to the pan. Cover the saucepan tightly. Simmer the stock 3–4 hours.
Strain the stock and cool it. Remove the fat when the stock is cold.

note: more water may be added to the bones and vegetables to make a 'second stock'. Simmer for a further 2–3 hours.

Fond blanc de volaille　Chicken stock

carcass of 1 cooked chicken
2 pints (5 cups) water
1 teaspoon salt
4 peppercorns
1 carrot
1 onion stuck with 4 cloves
1 stick celery
bouquet garni

Prepare the stock as for fond blanc (above). Break the chicken carcass into small pieces if necessary. Simmer for 1–1½ hours.

Court bouillon

1½ pints (3¾ cups) water
½ pint (1¼ cups) white wine
1 onion, sliced thinly
2 shallots, chopped
bouquet garni
1 teaspoon salt
6 white peppercorns

An aromatic liquor in which meat, fish and various vegetables are cooked.

Place all the ingredients into a saucepan. Cover, bring to the boil and simmer for 30–40 minutes. Strain.
Use as required.

note: the wine can be omitted and ¼ pint (⅝ cup) vinegar used instead.

Fond de poisson　Fish stock

Make the court bouillon as shown above but add a fish head and some bones to the saucepan.

Consommé

2 pints (5 cups) fond brun (beef bone stock)
2 egg whites
2 washed egg shells, crushed
4 oz. beef (lean shin is good), finely chopped
4 peppercorns
½ teaspoon salt
3 tablespoons (¼ cup) sherry
meat extract if necessary

serves 4

(Enriched, concentrated and clarified meat stock)
Allow the stock to become cold, then remove any fat.
Half whisk the egg whites.
Place the stock in a large saucepan and heat it slowly until nearly boiling.
Add the meat, egg whites, egg shells, peppercorns and salt. Bring the stock to the boil, whisking constantly with a fork or wire whisk. Simmer very gently, without whisking, for 1 hour. Strain through a scalded jelly (jello) cloth or bag into a scalded bowl. Add the sherry. The consommé should be a clear deep amber colour. A little meat extract can be used to adjust the colouring if necessary. Reheat, then add the chosen garnish. Serve very hot.

note: jelly (jello) cloths and bags can be bought from shops selling good kitchen equipment. Scald by pouring boiling water through.

Consommé brunoise

Beef bone consommé

1 tablespoon (1¼T) finely diced carrot
1 tablespoon (1¼T) finely diced turnip
1 tablespoon (1¼T) finely diced leek
1 tablespoon (1¼T) finely diced celery
1 quantity consommé
serves 4

Prepare the vegetables and cook in boiling water until tender.
Place a little of each vegetable in the bottom of 4 soup cups. Pour on piping hot consommé. Serve as soon as possible.

Consommé à la julienne

1 tablespoon (1¼T) matchstick shreds carrot
1 tablespoon (1¼T) matchstick shreds turnip
1 tablespoon (1¼T) matchstick shreds green leek
1 tablespoon (1¼T) matchstick shreds celery
1 quantity consommé
serves 4

Prepare and serve as for consommé brunoise.

Consommé au vermicelle

½ oz. vermicelli
1 quantity consommé
serves 4

Cook the vermicelli in boiling water until tender. Rinse well in hot water. Put a little vermicelli in each of 4 soup cups, pour in very hot consommé and serve as soon as possible.

Consommé en gelée

Cold jellied consommé

serves 4

Make the consommé as given above. When making the fond brun add a veal bone to the beef bones. Consommé gelée should gel on its own accord with no added gelatine. The veal bone will help in this.
Serve cold but not chilled, garnished with slices of lemon.

Consommé madrilène — Consommé with tomatoes

1 lb. red tomatoes
1 quantity consommé
½ oz. vermicelli, cooked
chervil

serves 4

Chop the tomatoes roughly and place them in a saucepan with a little water, if necessary. Heat until boiling, cook, stirring until the tomatoes are pulpy and leave the sides of the pan.
Make the consommé as shown above. Add the cooked tomatoes 15 minutes before the cooking time is completed. Strain in the usual way. Place a little vermicelli and a pinch of chervil in the bottom of each of 4 soup cups. Pour the hot consommé on top, serve as soon as possible.

Bisque de homard — Lobster bisque

1 large carrot
1 large onion
2 oz. (4T) butter
1 small lobster
3 tablespoons (¼ cup) brandy
½ pint (1¼ cups) white wine
4 oz. (½ cup) rice
3 pints (7½ cups) court bouillon
(see page 30)
¼ pint (⅝ cup) single (light) cream
salt and cayenne pepper
parsley for garnish

serves 6–8

Peel and chop the carrot and onion into small pieces. Melt 1 oz. butter in a large saucepan, add the vegetables and cook gently, stirring, 2–3 minutes. Split the lobster in half lengthways, remove the coral and place the lobster, cut side down, on the vegetables. Cover the pan, cook 2 minutes.
Heat the brandy, ignite and pour over the lobster with the wine. Cover the saucepan tightly and cook very gently for 15 minutes, lightly shaking the pan occasionally.
Cook the rice in 1 pint (2½ cups) boiling court bouillon for about 30 minutes or until very soft.
Shell the lobster, cut up the meat and place in a bowl with the coral, drained vegetables (reserve liquor), and rice. Pound very thoroughly to a soft pulp. (This can be done in an electric blender; add the reserved liquor for this process.) If done by hand, add the reserved liquor after the pounding is completed. Add ½ pint (1¼ cups) court bouillon and sieve.
Add the remaining court bouillon, pour into a clean saucepan. Reheat and whisk in the remaining 1 oz. butter in small pieces. Add the cream, then season with salt and cayenne pepper. Reheat, if necessary, without boiling.
Serve hot, garnished with a small sprig of parsley.

Potage à la hollandaise — Hollandaise soup

1 oz. (2T) butter
1 oz. (¼ cup) plain (all purpose) flour
1 pint (2½ cups) fond blanc (white stock)
1 onion
bouquet garni
1 egg yolk
¼ pint (⅝ cup) single (light) cream
cucumber, carrot, celery and peas for garnish

serves 4

Melt the butter in a saucepan, add the flour and cook gently, stirring constantly, until the roux has a 'honeycombed' appearance but is not browned. Add the stock and bring to the boil, stirring, then add the whole onion and the bouquet garni and simmer for 10–15 minutes. Remove the saucepan from the heat, cover and put aside for 10 minutes. Remove and discard the onion and bouquet garni. Mix the egg yolk with the cream, add to the soup and reheat very gently without boiling.
Cut the cucumber and carrot into small balls with a ball-cutter. Dice celery finely. Make about 1 tablespoon of each vegetable and add 1 tablespoon peas. Cook the carrot in boiling salted water for 2 minutes, add celery, cook another 3 minutes, add cucumber and peas and cook a further 2 minutes. Drain and rinse the vegetables in cold running water.
Add the garnish to the soup and reheat without boiling.
Serve piping hot.

French onion soup

Crème de concombres
Cream of cucumber soup

1 large cucumber
1 pint (2½ cups) fond brun (white stock)
¾ oz. (1½T) butter
¾ oz. (3 tablespoons) plain flour
3 tablespoons (¼ cup) milk
3 tablespoons (¼ cup) single (light) cream
salt and pepper
green colouring
watercress for garnish

Wash the cucumber. Removing about ¾ of the skin, chop the cucumber into large pieces. Bring a large saucepan of water to boiling point, add the cucumber, cook for 1 minute, then drain well. Pour the stock into a saucepan, add the cucumber and bring to the boil. Simmer, covered, for about 20 minutes or until the cucumber is very tender. Rub through a sieve or purée in an electric blender. Melt the butter in a clean saucepan, add the flour and cook, stirring constantly until the flour is cooked (the roux will have a 'honeycomb' appearance). Add the cucumber purée, bring to the boil, stirring constantly, and simmer 3–4 minutes.
Cool slightly, stir in the milk and cream. Season with salt and pepper to taste. Add a little green colouring if necessary. Reheat without boiling.

Serve very hot, garnished with sprigs of watercress or thin rounds of cucumber.

serves 4–6

note: Crème de Concombres can also be served chilled.

Soupe à l'oignon
French onion soup

1 lb. onions
2 oz. (¼ cup) butter
salt and black pepper
½ teaspoon mustard
2 teaspoons plain flour
1½ pints (3¾ cups) fond brun (beef bone stock)
¼ pint (⅝ cup) white wine
4–6 slices French bread, lightly toasted
2 oz. (½ cup) grated Parmesan cheese

serves 4–6

Peel and finely slice the onions. Melt the butter in a large saucepan, then add the onion rings, salt, pepper and mustard. Cook over a very gentle heat, stirring occasionally until onion is browned (this will take 20–30 minutes).
Add the flour and stir until smooth. Add the stock and white wine, stirring constantly, then bring to the boil and simmer for 30 minutes. Taste and adjust seasoning.
Place slices of toasted bread on the bottom of a soup tureen or in individual soup bowls, sprinkling with cheese. Pour hot soup carefully on to bread.
Place under a hot grill until the cheese is beginning to brown.
Serve immediately.

Crème vichyssoise Cold leek soup

1 lb. potatoes
4 leeks (white part only)
1 onion
2 oz. (4T) butter
2½ pints (6¼ cups) fond blanc (white stock)
¼ pint (⅝ cup) double (heavy) cream
1 tablespoon snipped chives
pinch of nutmeg
salt and pepper to taste
serves 4–6

Prepare the vegetables, slice thinly.
Melt the butter in a large saucepan, then add the leeks and the onion. Fry, stirring, until softened. Add the stock and the potatoes, bring to the boil, cover the pan and simmer for 30–40 minutes. Press the soup through a sieve with a wooden spoon, or purée in an electric blender. Allow to become quite cold.
Stir in the cream and chives. Season with nutmeg and salt and pepper to taste. Add a little extra stock if the soup is too thick.
Serve cold in chilled soup cups.

Garbure Classic peasant vegetable soup

2 carrots
2 onions
1 small turnip
¼ cabbage
2 leeks
4 sticks celery
2 potatoes
1 oz. (2T) butter
2 tablespoons (2½T) olive oil
7 oz. (1 cup) cooked
haricot beans
4 pints (10 cups) fond brun
(beef bone stock)
6 slices French bread
2 oz. (½ cup) grated
gruyère cheese
salt and pepper
serves 6

Prepare the fresh vegetables and slice thinly. Melt the butter with 1 tablespoon (1¼T) of olive oil in a large saucepan, then add the prepared vegetables. Cover the saucepan and cook very gently for 20–25 minutes. Add the beans and stock. Cover the saucepan, bring to the boil and simmer 20–30 minutes or until vegetables are very tender. Press the soup through a sieve with a wooden spoon or purée in an electric blender. Return it to the saucepan and continue simmering, uncovered, until it begins to thicken.
Heat the remaining 1 tablespoon (1¼T) oil in a small frying pan and fry the slices of bread until golden on both sides. Spread each slice with a little soup and sprinkle with cheese.
Season the soup. Pour into a soup tureen or on to individual soup plates. Serve piping hot topped with the croûtes of bread and cheese.

Purée de tomate Thick tomato soup

2 lb. tomatoes
1 oz. (2T) butter
1 oz. bacon, chopped
1 onion, chopped
1 carrot, chopped
1 stick celery, chopped
2 pints (7 cups) fond blanc
(white stock)
1 bayleaf
10 white peppercorns
3 tablespoons (¼ cup)
cornflour (cornstarch)
3 tablespoons (¼ cup) milk
1 tablespoon (1¼T) single
(light) cream
salt and sugar to taste
finely chopped parsley for garnish
serves 4–6

Wash the tomatoes and chop them roughly. Melt the butter in a large saucepan, add the bacon and fry until softened. Add the onion, carrot and celery and fry gently until softened but not browned. Add the tomatoes, stock, bayleaf and peppercorns. Bring to the boil and simmer very gently in an uncovered pan for 1½ hours.
Sieve the soup, pressing it through the sieve well with a wooden spoon. Mix the cornflour with the milk. Place the tomato purée and cornflour in a clean saucepan, bring to the boil and simmer 3–4 minutes, stirring constantly. Add the cream, taste and adjust seasoning, adding salt and sugar as necessary.
Reheat without boiling. Serve piping hot, garnishing with chopped parsley.

Velouté de volaille Creamed chicken soup

1 pint (2½ cups) fond blanc de
volaille (chicken stock)
½ oz. (2 tablespoons)
cornflour (cornstarch)
¼ pint (⅝ cup) milk
2 egg yolks
3 tablespoons (¼ cup) double
(heavy) cream
nutmeg, salt and pepper
1 breast of chicken, cooked
serves 4

Strain the stock, pour it into a saucepan and bring it to the boil. Mix the cornflour with the milk and gradually add to the stock. Re-boil, then cook 2–3 minutes.
Mix the egg yolks with the cream, adding the nutmeg, salt and pepper. Add to the saucepan, reheat and cook gently until it begins to thicken, without boiling.
Cut the chicken breast into julienne strips, and add to the soup. Adjust seasoning.
Serve in a hot tureen or individual soup cups.

Preparing and chopping the leeks

Cold leek soup

Eggs, pancakes and savoury pastries

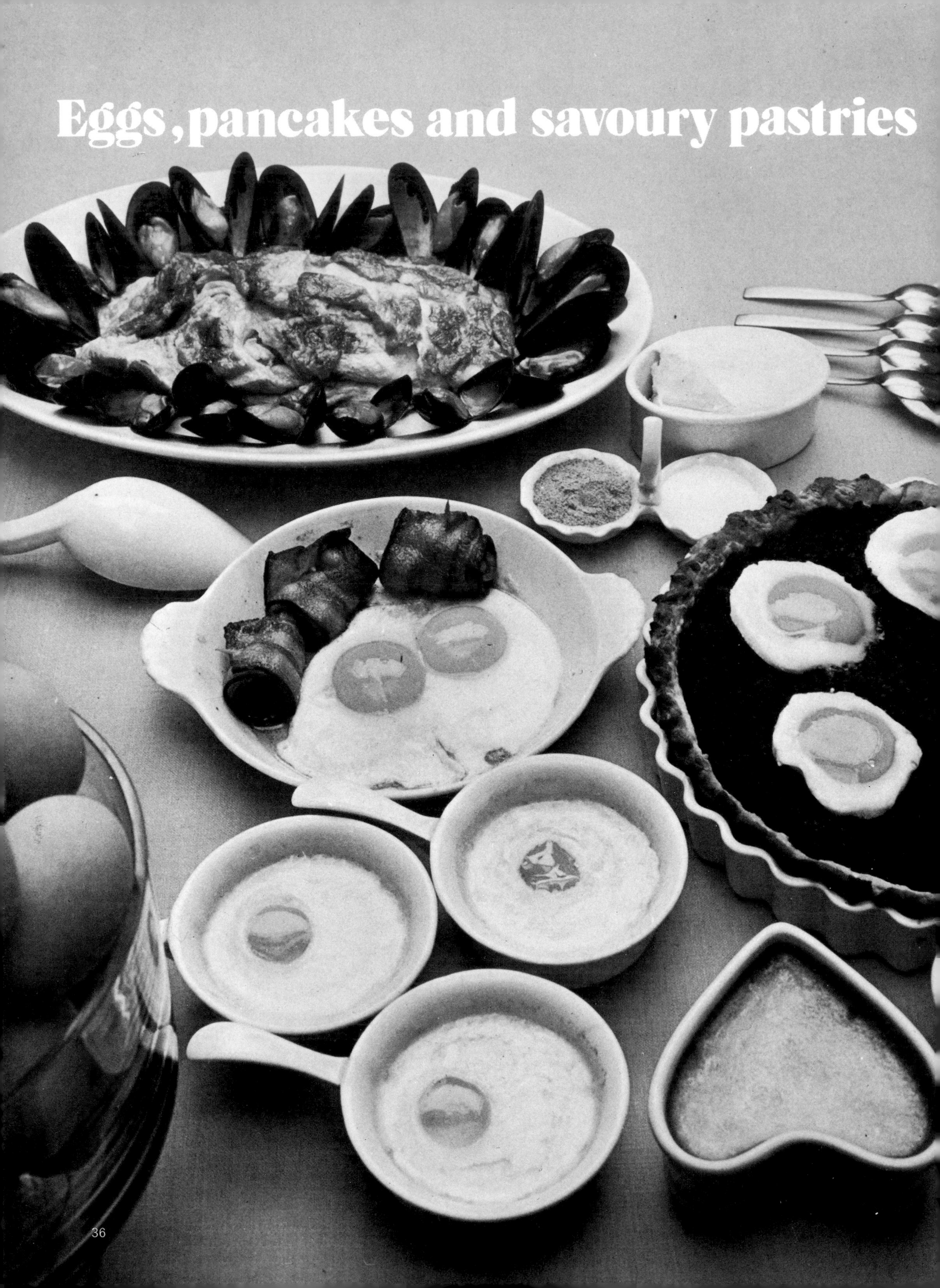

Eggs play a tremendous part in French cuisine. They are
not necessarily served at breakfast time (we all know that
a French petit déjeuner consists of a large cup of coffee
and rolls and butter) but are sometimes served for lunch
or supper or as part of a dinner party menu.
Omelettes, soufflés, pancakes and savoury flans can all be
served as hors d'oeuvres. They also make a superb
luncheon if teamed with crisp French bread, a green
salad with homemade mayonnaise and perhaps a
steaming hot bowl of soup to start.
The number of recipes is endless, but all of them produce
a light dish, under rather than overcooked and extremely
nutritious.

A selection of egg dishes

Oeufs au beurre noir

Fried eggs with black butter

4 oz. (8T) butter
4 eggs
½ tablespoon (¾T) wine vinegar
1 tablespoon (1¼T) finely chopped parsley

serves 4

Melt 3 oz. (6T) butter in a frying pan. Break the eggs into the pan and cook gently, basting the eggs with the butter to cook the tops. Place the cooked eggs on a heated serving plate. Add the remaining butter to the pan and cook until a deep brown (be careful it does not burn). Add vinegar and parsley, stirring quickly, then pour over eggs. Serve immediately.

Oeufs sur le plat

Eggs cooked on a plate

2 oz. (4T) butter
4 eggs

This dish is traditionally cooked in a shallow copper or earthenware dish with handles or 'ears'. There are innumerable variations on the basic recipe. Serve as a light lunch or supper dish.

Melt 1 oz. (2T) of the butter in a heatproof dish (individual dishes can also be used), and heat until sizzling. Melt the remaining butter in a small saucepan.
Break each egg carefully into the heatproof dish and spoon a little melted butter over each yolk. Bake in a very hot oven (450°F. Mark 7) for 3–4 minutes or until the whites are just set and the yolks still runny.

serves 4

Serve immediately.

Niçoise

Chop roughly 2 sticks celery, 2 tomatoes (skinned and deseeded) and 2 anchovies. Cook with 1 tablespoon olive oil in the heatproof dish, until softened. Add eggs and bake as above.

Bercy

Cook eggs as above. Pour over a little sauce bercy (see recipe page 20) and serve immediately.

Lorraine

Remove the rind and rust from 2 rashers of bacon. Cut into dice and cook in boiling water for 3–4 minutes. Heat the butter in the base of the heatproof dish, add a layer of bacon then a layer of 1 oz. grated gruyère cheese. Add the eggs, pour the melted butter over, season. Bake for 5–7 minutes in a moderate oven (350°F. Mark 4).

note: for a richer dish, substitute a teaspoonful of cream for the melted butter poured over the egg yolks.

Eggs Lorraine

Oeufs florentine
Eggs with spinach

12 oz. (1½ cups) frozen or cooked spinach
½ oz. (1T) butter
salt, pepper and ground nutmeg
oil for frying
6 eggs
½ pint (1¼ cups) sauce mornay (see recipe page 17)

Cook the spinach in the minimum of water, in a large saucepan. Drain very thoroughly, beat in the butter and season to taste. Heat a little oil in a frying pan, add an egg and fry it gently, spooning a little of the hot oil over the yolk to set the top. Remove and drain well. Cook all the remaining eggs in the same way. Place the eggs carefully on the spinach in a heatproof serving dish. Coat the entire dish with the prepared sauce mornay. Grill quickly under a hot grill until beginning to brown. Serve immediately.

variations: use other bases under the fried eggs. Oeufs Niçoise and Oeufs Lorraine can be made using the ingredients given as variations in Oeufs sur la Plat and using them as above. If you like, sprinkle extra grated cheese on the top before grilling.

serves 6

Oeufs en cocotte à la crème
Eggs baked with cream

4 tablespoons (5T) cream
8 eggs
½ oz. (1T) butter
salt
freshly ground black pepper

Cook these eggs in individual heatproof dishes or 'cocottes'.

Heat the cream in a small saucepan until boiling. Warm the cocottes and pour 1 tablespoon (1¼T) of cream into each. Add the eggs carefully (2 to each cocotte) so as not to break the yolks. Dot each egg with small pieces of butter. Season. Stand the cocottes in a roasting pan with hot water coming halfway up the sides. Cover with aluminium foil. Bake in a moderate oven (350°F. Mark 4) for 6–8 minutes or until the whites are set and the yolks are creamy. Serve immediately.

serves 4

Oeufs au gratin
Eggs baked with breadcrumbs and ham

2 oz. ham
4 tablespoons (good ¼ cup) fresh white breadcrumbs
salt and freshly ground black pepper
¼ teaspoon dry mustard
1 oz. (2T) butter
1 tablespoon (1¼T) hot milk
4 eggs

Chop the ham and mix with the breadcrumbs and seasonings. Melt ½ oz. of the butter and add it to the ham mixture with the milk. Mix well. Reserve 2 tablespoons (2½T) of the ham mixture, then place the remainder in the base of a heatproof dish. Make four indentations and break an egg carefully into each. Scatter reserved mixture on top. Dot with small pieces of remaining butter. Bake in a moderate oven (350°F. Mark 4) for 5–7 minutes or until eggs are set. Serve immediately.

serves 4

Oeufs brouillés aux tomates
Scrambled eggs with tomatoes

2 tomatoes
1 tablespoon (1¼T) olive oil
1 shallot, finely chopped
1 oz. (2T) butter
1 tablespoon (1¼T) milk
4 eggs
salt and pepper
chopped parsley for garnish

Blanche the tomatoes in boiling water, remove skin and pips. Chop roughly. Heat the olive oil in a small saucepan, fry the shallot until it has softened then add the tomatoes. Cook for 2–3 minutes, stirring constantly. Melt the butter in a saucepan. Beat the milk and eggs together and season. Add the eggs to the butter and cook, stirring constantly over a low heat, until the mixture is creamy. Place the scrambled eggs on a heated dish, make a hollow in the centre. Spoon the tomato mixture on to the eggs and garnish with finely chopped parsley. Serve immediately.

serves 4

Oeufs mollets à la crécy
Soft-boiled eggs with carrots

3 carrots
2 oz. (4T) butter
½ pint (1¼ cups) sauce béchamel
(see recipe page 16)
4 eggs
salt and pepper
2 tablespoons fresh white
breadcrumbs
1 tablespoon (1¼T) melted butter

Oeufs mollets can be served in many ways. 'A la Crécy' they make a good light supper dish or can be served as an appetizer.

Peel the carrots and grate. Place the butter in a small saucepan, melt it gently then add the prepared carrot. Cover pan and cook very, very gently for 10–15 minutes or until the carrot is soft. Prepare sauce béchamel.
Boil a large saucepan of water. Add the eggs (in their shells) and cook them for exactly 4 minutes. Immerse them in cold water. Carefully remove the egg shells.
Season the carrots and place an equal amount in each of four small individual heatproof dishes. Place the cooked eggs on top and coat with the sauce béchamel. Sprinkle the breadcrumbs on the sauce and pour a little melted butter over.
Place dishes under a very hot grill until tops are lightly tinted brown. Serve immediately.

serves 4

Piperade
Basque egg and vegetables

12 oz. tomatoes
2 green peppers
1 shallot
2 tablespoons (scant ¼ cup)
olive oil
2 cloves garlic, crushed
4 eggs
3 tablespoons (¼ cup) milk
salt and pepper
4 rounds fried bread
serves 4–6

Skin the tomatoes, remove the seeds and chop. Remove seeds and membranes from the peppers and cut into dice. Peel and chop the shallot finely. Heat the olive oil and fry the shallot and garlic until beginning to colour. Add the peppers, cook gently for 4–5 minutes. Add the tomato and simmer uncovered until the tomato is pulpy, stirring occasionally.
Beat the eggs and milk together, season, add them to saucepan and cook gently, stirring, for 2–4 minutes or until the eggs are creamy. Spoon the egg mixture on to the rounds of fried bread. Serve immediately on a heated serving plate.

Crêpes
Pancakes

4 oz. (1 cup) plain (all
purpose) flour
salt
1 egg
½ pint (1¼ cups) milk
4 tablespoons (¼–½ cup) clarified
butter or lard

Savoury crêpes are made from exactly the same pancake batter as sweet crêpes. They can be served with a wide variety of fillings as appetizers or for a light lunch or supper dish.

Sift the flour with a pinch of salt into a mixing bowl. Make a well in the centre and add the egg. Using a wooden spoon, mix the egg and gradually incorporate the flour from around the well. Beat, adding the milk gradually until all the flour is blended. Stir in the remaining milk.
Heat about ½ tablespoon clarified butter in a 7 inch diameter frying pan. Drain off excess.
Add about 1 large tablespoon of batter to the frying pan, tilting pan to spread the batter evenly and cook until the surface is bubbly.
Slide a palette knife under the crêpe, loosen and then turn it over. Cook until underside is lightly browned.
Cool the cooked crêpes on a clean tea towel. They can be stacked in piles of 4 or 6 for storage in the refrigerator and also freeze well if required.

makes about 8×7 inch crêpes

Crêpes florentine   Pancakes with spinach

8 cooked crêpes (see above)
2 onions, finely chopped
2 rashers streaky bacon,
cut into strips
1½ oz. (3T) butter
1 × 14 oz. packet frozen
chopped spinach
1 oz. (¼ cup) plain (all
purpose) flour
¼ pint (⅝ cup) milk
2 tablespoons (2½T) single
(light) cream
salt and pepper

serves 4

Prepare the crêpes.
Place the onion, bacon and ½ oz. (1T) of the butter in a saucepan.
Fry until the onion and bacon are softened. Add the frozen spinach,
cover pan tightly and cook for 5 minutes on a high heat. Uncover,
stir and cook for a further 4 minutes, stirring occasionally until dry.
(It will hiss loudly when sufficiently dry.)
Melt the remaining 1 oz. (2T) butter in a clean saucepan, stir in the
flour and cook for 2 minutes. Remove from the heat and add the milk
gradually, stirring constantly. Return to the heat, bring to the boil
and boil for 2 minutes, stirring constantly. Add the prepared spinach
mixture with the cream. Season to taste and combine thoroughly.
Place the filling on the crêpes, down the middle. Roll up carefully.
Serve immediately or reheat by placing the crêpes in an ovenproof
dish, cover with foil and place in a moderate oven (350°F. Mark 4) for
15 minutes.

Crêpes aux crevettes provençale   Prawn pancakes provençale

8 cooked crêpes (see above)
1 onion, finely chopped
1 oz. (2T) butter
1 green pepper, chopped
8 oz. tomatoes, skinned and
chopped
6 oz. peeled prawns (shrimp)
1 clove garlic, crushed
salt and freshly ground
black pepper
6 black olives, pitted
serves 4

Prepare the crêpes.
Place the onion and butter in a small saucepan. Fry the onion gently
until softened. Add the pepper and continue cooking for 5 minutes.
Add the tomatoes, prawns (shrimp), garlic and seasonings. Cover the
cook gently for 10 minutes.
Place the filling equally on each cool or cold pancake. Roll up and
place in a greased ovenproof dish. Cover with foil and cook in a
moderate oven (350°F. Mark 4) for 15 minutes.
Serve garnished with chopped black olives.

Crêpes aux rognons   Kidney pancakes

8 cooked crêpes (see above)
4 lambs' kidneys
6 rashers streaky bacon
oil if necessary
1 onion, thinly sliced
½ oz. (2 tablespoons) plain (all
purpose) flour
¼ pint (⅝ cup) chicken soup
salt and freshly ground
black pepper
1 tablespoon (1¼T)
tomato paste
1 tablespoon (1¼T) sherry
¼ teaspoon chopped dried basil
chopped parsley and bacon rolls
(rashers of bacon rolled up and
secured with a toothpick)
for garnish
serves 4

Prepare the crêpes.
Skin the kidneys, remove the cores and slice thinly. Remove the
rind from the bacon and cut into dice. Fry the bacon in a saucepan
until golden. Remove, add the kidneys and cook quickly for 2–3
minutes, remove. Add a little oil if necessary, fry the onion until
browned, sprinkle with the flour and continue cooking for 2–3
minutes, stirring constantly. Add stock, bring to the boil and simmer
for 1 minute. Add all the remaining ingredients (except garnish) to
the pan, including the bacon and kidneys, bring to the boil, cover
and simmer for 15–20 minutes.
Place the filling equally on each cooled or cold crêpe. Roll each
crêpe and place in an ovenproof dish. Cover with aluminium foil and
reheat in a moderate oven (350°F Mark 4) for 15 minutes.
Serve garnished with chopped parsley and grilled bacon rolls.

Cooking an omelette
(a) With a fork the egg mixture is drawn from the sides to the middle of the pan, allowing the omelette to cook quickly.

(b) The cooked omelette is folded over in half, then gently shaken out on to a heated plate.

Omelette

2 eggs
1 tablespoon (1¼T) water
salt and pepper
½ oz. (1T) butter

Break the eggs into a bowl and whisk very lightly with a fork until the whites and yolks are mixed but not frothy. Stir in the water and seasonings.

Melt the butter in an omelette pan (use one with a 6 inch diameter base) and heat until just beginning to brown. Add the egg mixture and cook rapidly, using a fork to stir the mixture. Bring some of the cooked mixture to the centre, allowing the uncooked egg to come into contact with the pan. Continue cooking until the top is lightly set and the underside is a light golden brown. Fold the omelette in half, slide it on to a heated serving plate.
Serve immediately.

serves 1

note: a filling is frequently added to an omelette just before it is folded. An omelette 'aux fines herbes' however has the chopped mixed herbs actually added to the egg mixture before cooking.

Omelette au fromage

Cheese omelette

Add 1 oz. (¼ cup) finely grated cheese to the omelette, just before folding.

Omelette au jambon et champignon

Ham and mushroom omelette

Melt ½ oz. (1T) butter in a small saucepan, add 1 oz. (¼ cup) finely diced ham, fry for 2–3 minutes. Wash 1 oz. button mushrooms, slice thinly, add to the pan and continue cooking for a further 2–3 minutes. Season to taste, add 1 teaspoon finely chopped parsley. Add filling to the omelette just before folding.

Omelette parmentier

Potato omelette

Cut a small cooked potato into thin slices. Melt 1 oz. (2T) butter in a frying pan and fry potato until crisp and golden. Sprinkle with ¼ teaspoon chopped dried rosemary. Add to the omelette just before folding.

Omelette aux crevettes

Prawn (shrimp) omelette

Prepare the prawn (shrimp) filling as for Crêpes aux Crevettes Provençales. Add the filling to the omelette just before folding.

Soufflé au fromage   Cheese soufflé

2½ oz. (5T) butter
2 tablespoons (2½T) fresh white breadcrumbs
1½ oz. (⅜ cup) plain (all purpose) flour
scant ½ pint (1⅛ cups) milk
4 egg yolks
2 oz. (½ cup) grated Parmesan cheese
1 oz. (¼ cup) grated gruyère cheese
pinch cayenne pepper
pinch freshly ground black pepper
½ teaspoon salt
5 egg whites

serves 4

Using ½ oz. (1T) of the butter, grease a 6 inch soufflé dish. Cut a double strip of greaseproof paper, long enough to go around the soufflé dish and wide enough to stand 2 inches above the edge of the dish. Grease the top 2 inches of one side of the paper. Tie the paper around the dish, greased side inside. Sprinkle the breadcrumbs around the inside of the dish.

Melt the remaining butter in a saucepan, add the flour and cook gently, stirring constantly for 2–3 minutes until 'honeycombed' in appearance but not browned. Add milk, bring to the boil, stirring constantly and simmer 2–3 minutes. Cool slightly, beat in the egg yolks one at a time, then add the grated cheeses and seasonings. Whisk the egg whites until they stand in stiff peaks. Beat 1 tablespoon (1¼T) egg white into the saucepan mixture. Then gently fold in the remaining egg whites.

Pour the soufflé mixture into the prepared dish.

Bake in a moderately hot oven (375°F. Mark 5) for 35–40 minutes or until well risen, firm and golden. Remove greasproof paper. Serve immediately.

Soufflé aux épinards   Spinach soufflé

Omit cheeses, breadcrumbs and cayenne pepper. Use instead 1 lb. spinach (cooked, well-drained and very finely chopped), 2 oz. (½ cup) grated gruyère cheese, 1 shallot (peeled and grated), and ¼ teaspoon grated nutmeg.

Soufflé aux champignons   Mushroom soufflé

Omit breadcrumbs, gruyère cheese and cayenne pepper. Use instead 8 oz. mushrooms (finely chopped and sautéd in a little butter), 1 shallot (peeled and grated), 1 teaspoon lemon juice and ¼ teaspoon grated nutmeg.

Making a soufflé
(a) Milk is added to a mixture of flour and melted butter.
(b) The egg yolks, grated cheeses and seasoning are gradually added.
(c) The egg whites are whisked until very stiff, then folded into the sauce mixture.
(d) The mixture is poured into the prepared soufflé dish, three-quarters filling it, then baked in the oven.
(e) The finished soufflé should be well risen, firm and golden.

a

b

c

d

e

Quiche lorraine
Cheese, egg and bacon flan

4 oz. pâte brisée (see recipe page 119)
2 eggs
2 oz. (½ cup) grated gruyère cheese
¼ pint (⅝ cup) single (light) cream
salt and pepper
1 oz. (2T) butter
4 rashers streaky bacon, diced
1 onion, finely sliced
serves 4–6

Make the pastry and line a 7 inch diameter plain flan ring standing on a baking tray.
Beat the eggs and cheese together with the cream, salt and pepper.
Melt the butter in a frying pan and fry the bacon and onion until beginning to brown.
Spread the bacon and onion over the base of the uncooked flan, then pour in the egg and cream mixture. Bake in a moderate oven (350°F. Mark 4) for 20–25 minutes or until golden brown and firm to the touch.
Serve immediately, while still puffed up.

Tarte à l'oignon Onion tart

4 oz. pâté brisée (see recipe
page 119)
1½ lb. onions
2 eggs
1 egg yolk
¼ pint (⅝ cup) single cream
¼ teaspoon grated nutmeg
¼ teaspoon freshly ground
black pepper
2 oz. (4T) butter
1 tablespoon olive oil
ham for garnish

serves 4–6

This dish is from Alsace.

Make the pastry and line a 7 inch diameter plain flan ring standing on a baking tray.
Peel the onions and slice very thinly. Beat together the eggs, egg yolk, cream and seasonings.
Heat the butter and oil in a saucepan, add the onions and cook (very gently), uncovered, until soft and golden. This must be done very slowly to prevent the onions from burning. Stir occasionally. Mix the onions into the cream mixture, then spoon into the prepared uncooked flan case. Bake in a moderate oven (350°F. Mark 4) for about 30 minutes or until well risen and browned.
Serve immediately, garnished with strips of thinly sliced ham.

Gougère au poulet et jambon Cheese choux pastry flan with chicken and ham

¼ pint (⅝ cup) water
2 oz. (4T) butter
2½ oz. (good ½ cup) plain (all
purpose) flour
2 eggs
2 oz. (½ cup) coarsely grated
gruyère cheese
salt and pepper
1½ tablespoons (⅛ cup) olive oil
2 shallots, chopped
2 mushrooms, chopped
extra ½ tablespoon plain (all
purpose) flour
¼ pint (1¼ cups) chicken stock
4 oz. (1 cup) chopped
cooked chicken
2 oz. (½ cup) chopped
cooked ham
1 tomato, skinned and chopped
1 tablespoon (1¼T) grated
Parmesan cheese
1 tablespoon (1¼T) brown
breadcrumbs
1 teaspoon finely
chopped parsley
serves 4–6

Gougère is a dish from the Burgundy region of France. It has become very popular and is now made in all parts of the country.

Place the water and butter in a saucepan, heat until the butter is melted and the water is boiling. Add the flour, off the heat, and beat until the mixture is smooth.
Allow the mixture to cool, then add the eggs one at a time. Beat very well after each addition. Continue beating until the mixture is smooth. Add the gruyère cheese and mix well. Season. Place the olive oil in a saucepan, add the shallots and fry them until softened. Add the mushrooms and cook for 2 minutes. Add the extra flour, cook, stirring constantly 2–3 minutes. Add the stock, bring to the boil and simmer for 5 minutes. Add chicken, ham and tomato.
Arrange the cheese choux pastry in spoonfuls around a greased ovenproof dish. Pile the filling into the centre, sprinkle with Parmesan cheese and breadcrumbs.
Bake in a hot oven (400°F. Mark 6) for 30–40 minutes or until well risen, golden, firm to the touch and cooked through. (Avoid opening the oven door before 30 minutes is up).
Serve as soon as possible, garnished with chopped parsley.

Croque monsieur Cheese toasted sandwich

2 thin slices bread (from a
sandwich loaf)
½ oz. (1T) butter
1 slice gruyère cheese
1 slice cooked ham
clarified butter for frying
serves 1

Serve this as an easily prepared snack or an unusual appetizer.

Remove crusts from the slices of bread. Butter both on one side only. Place the gruyère cheese on the buttered side of one piece of bread, top with the ham and cover with the second slice of bread. Fry the sandwich in hot clarified butter until it is golden. Drain well and serve very hot.

Quiche Lorraine

Fish

Fish has always played a large part in French cooking; the French border is three quarters sea and there are also a great number of inland rivers and waterways rich in fish. Atlantic, Mediterranean and fresh water fish are all popular, especially in the local areas, for it is important that the fish be cooked when at its freshest.

Whether fish is being prepared for an extra special dinner party or simply for the family, the method of cooking is always simple. Fish is extremely nutritious and as tender as the finest beef steak. Long cooking is unnecessary and in fact would spoil the fish. Some of the most famous methods of cooking fish come from France, for instance 'à la meunière' and 'moules marinière'. There are also some great French classic fish dishes such as bouillabaisse and la bourride which, although difficult to make without Mediterranean fish, can be copied with reasonable success.

Fish can only be kept successfully for a very short time unless frozen. Frozen fish can be very good, since it is frozen immediately the catch is in and all the flavour, texture and goodness are preserved. Only freeze your own fish if they are very fresh indeed. Preparing fish can be a laborious and difficult job. Ask your fishmonger to clean, skin and fillet your purchase (as necessary). After all, he is the expert.

Filets de merlan à la meunière
Fillets of whiting meunière

4×12 oz. whiting
4 oz. (8T) clarified butter
flour
salt and pepper
1 egg, beaten
2 teaspoons chopped parsley
1 tablespoon (1¼T) lemon juice

serves 4

Fillet the fish:— Remove the heads and fins along the sides and bottom of the fish. Insert a very sharp knife to one side of the backbone and with long smooth cuts, ease the fillet away from the bones. Turn the fish over and remove the other fillet. Trim. Clarify the butter. Mix the flour with a little salt and pepper. Dip the fillets in the flour and then into the beaten egg. Heat the butter in a large frying pan and fry the fillets until golden brown on both sides, turning once.

Place the whiting on a heated serving plate. Pour off all the butter in the pan except 2 tablespoons (2½T), add the parsley and lemon juice, reheat and pour over fish. Serve immediately.

La brandade de morue
Creamed cod

1 lb. dried salt cod (or 1½ lb. fresh cod, tablespoon (1¼T) salt and 1 teaspoon lemon juice)
½ pint (1¼ cups) sauce béchamel (see recipe page 16)
8 fluid oz. (1 cup) olive oil
1 small clove garlic, crushed
freshly ground black pepper
croûtes of fried bread

serves 6

This is a traditional dish from the Mediterranean. It is a speciality of both Languedoc and Provence. Unfortunately, due to the long preparation, it is not made in the home as frequently as it used to be, but is bought ready made. If you own an electric mixer or blender, however, this certainly takes all the hard work out of this recipe. Use 1½ lbs. fresh cod if the dried salt cod is not available.

Soak the dried salt cod in cold water for 24 hours, changing the water once. Rinse well. Place in a large saucepan, cover with fresh cold water, bring to the boil and simmer for 30 minutes. (Fresh cod must be sprinkled with salt, left for 30 minutes and then, after the excess liquid and salt have been removed, covered and baked in a moderate oven (350°F. Mark 4) for 15–20 minutes.) Prepare the sauce béchamel and keep warm. Heat the olive oil gently in a small pan until almost boiling.

Beat the cooked cod with the garlic until smooth. This is a laborious and long job when done by hand but can be done with equal success in a mixer. It can also be successfully done in an electric blender. Add a little of the sauce béchamel when you begin to moisten it. When smooth, and all the fish fibres have been broken down, add about 3 tablespoons (3¾T) sauce béchamel, continue beating and add 3 tablespoons olive oil. Continue in this way until all the sauce and the oil are smoothly blended in. Season with black pepper. Reheat, serve in a heated dish, surrounded with fried croûtes of bread.

Thon à la provençale
Tuna fish Provençale

2×7 oz. cans tuna
juice of ½ lemon
salt and freshly ground
black pepper
4 anchovy fillets
1 tablespoon olive oil
1 onion, chopped
4 ripe tomatoes, skinned, deseeded and chopped
1 clove garlic, crushed
bouquet garni
¼ pint (⅝ cup) white wine
chopped parsley for garnish

serves 4

Tuna fish are found in both the Mediterranean Sea and the Atlantic Ocean, off the French coast. If you are lucky enough to be able to get fresh fish, use a middle cut, marinate it in olive oil, then continue with the following recipe.

Remove the tuna from the cans very carefully so that they stay in shape and place side by side on an ovenproof serving dish. Sprinkle them with the lemon juice and season lightly with salt and pepper. Arrange the anchovy fillets on the top.

Heat the olive oil in a small saucepan, add the onion and cook until softened. Add tomatoes, garlic, a bouquet garni and wine. Bring to the boil and boil rapidly, uncovered, until reduced and thickened. Pour the sauce over the tuna, cover and bake in a moderate oven (350°F. Mark 4) for 10–15 minutes. Remove bouquet garni. Serve sprinkled with chopped parsley.

Trout with almonds

Filets de plie mornay Plaice fillets in cheese sauce

2×12 oz. plaice
court bouillon (see recipe
page 30)
1 slice lemon
½ pint (1¼ cups) sauce mornay
(see recipe page 17)
grated Parmesan cheese

serves 4

Skin the plaice, fillet and cut each fillet in half lengthwise. Fold the pieces of fish in three and place them in a greased ovenproof dish. Add the court bouillon to a depth of ½ inch and the lemon slice. Cover and bake in a moderate oven (350°F. Mark 4) for 10–15 minutes. Drain the fillets.
Arrange the cooked plaice in a heated serving dish. Make the sauce mornay and coat the fish with it. Sprinkle the top with Parmesan cheese and place under a hot grill until the cheese is melted. The top may be browned if you prefer, but this is not essential. Serve very hot.

Plaice fillets in cheese sauce (above)   Herrings Brittany-style (right)

Filets de sole orly Fillets of sole Orly

4 sole fillets

marinade
1 tablespoon (1¼T) olive oil
½ tablespoon (⅔T)
tarragon vinegar
1 teaspoon lemon juice
1 teaspoon chopped parsley
1 teaspoon finely chopped shallot
pinch each of cayenne pepper
and salt

batter
2 eggs
2 oz. (½ cup) plain (all
purpose) flour
salt
2 tablespoons milk
1 tablespoon (1¼T) oil
oil for deep frying
sauce de tomate Provençale
(see recipe page 20)
for serving
serves 4

Wipe the fillets, skin them, cut in half lengthwise then each half into thirds, diagonally.

Mix all the marinade ingredients together, add the sole pieces and marinate for 30 minutes.

Separate eggs. Sift the flour and salt into a mixing bowl, add egg yolks, milk and oil, beating well all the time. Whisk egg whites until stiff and fold into the batter just before using.

Heat oil for deep frying until 375°F. (a ¼ inch dice of bread will brown in less than a minute). Dip marinated sole pieces in the batter and deep fry until golden. Drain well on absorbent kitchen paper. Serve hot. Serve tomato sauce separately.

note: if sole is not available, use flounder or plaice fillets.

Filets de sole Veronique
Fillets of sole with grapes

2×12 oz. lemon or Dover sole
salt and freshly ground
black pepper
4 oz. white grapes
¾ pint (scant 2 cups) sauce
velouté (see recipe page 19)
paprika pepper for garnish

Skin and fillet the soles. Place bones and skin in a saucepan with 1 pint (2½ cups) water. Bring to the boil, covered, and simmer for 30 minutes. Strain.

Cut each fillet in half down the centre lengthwise and season well. Fold in 3, skin side inside. Place in a greased ovenproof dish with the prepared fish stock. Cover and bake in a moderate oven (350°F. Mark 4) for 15 minutes.

Drain the sole, keeping hot, and pour the stock into a saucepan. Boil the stock rapidly until reduced to 2 or 3 tablespoons (2½ or 3¾T). Make the sauce velouté and add the reduced fish stock. Skin and depip the grapes, heat in a little water.

Arrange the fish on a heated serving dish, coat with the sauce and garnish with the hot grapes. Sprinkle a little paprika pepper on top of each sole fillet.

serves 4

note: white wine may be used instead of fish stock and for heating the grapes. Use plaice or flounder if sole is not available.

Sole à la colbert
Fried sole with maître d'hôtel butter

4×8 oz. soles
flour
salt and pepper
lemon juice
2 eggs, beaten
fine white dried breadcrumbs
oil for deep frying
sprigs of parsley
2 thin slices lemon
2 oz. (4T) maître d'hôtel butter

Wash, clean and skin the soles, leaving the heads on. On the 'white' side, make a cut down the centre to the bone, 1 inch in from the top and bottom. Carefully slice the fish away from the bones on each side and roll the flesh of the fillet back. Using scissors, carefully snip through the rib bones in the opening. Mix the flour with salt and pepper. Sprinkle the soles with lemon juice and coat in seasoned flour.

Dip each sole carefully in beaten egg and then coat in the breadcrumbs. Heat the oil for frying to 375°F. (a ¼ inch slice of bread will brown in less than a minute). Deep fry the soles, one at a time, until golden. Drain well on absorbent kitchen paper. Remove the bones from the opening.

Fry dry sprigs of parsley until they are crisp, about 30 seconds. Serve the soles on a heated dish, then put the fried parsley and maître d'hôtel butter in the opening. Garnish with lemon butterflies.

serves 4

Maître d'hôtel butter

Cream 2 oz. (4T) butter with a wooden spoon until soft. Add 2 teaspoons lemon juice and 2 teaspoons of finely chopped parsley with salt and pepper. Beat well until they have thoroughly combined. Make into a long 'sausage', wrap in aluminium foil and chill until needed.

Fillets of sole Orly

Sole normande   Sole Normandy-style

4 sole fillets
¼ pint (⅝ cup) cider (hard)
¼ pint (⅝ cup) water
salt and pepper
2 oz. button mushrooms
2 oz. (4T) butter
1 oz. (¼ cup) plain (all purpose) flour
1 egg yolk
1 teaspoon lemon juice
12 mussels, cooked
watercress for garnish

Wipe the fillets, skin them and cut in half down the centre. Fold each piece of fish in half and place it in a greased ovenproof dish. Add the (hard) cider and the water and season. Cover and bake in a moderate oven (350°F. Mark 4) for 15–20 minutes. Drain and keep hot, reserving the cooking liquor (liquid).

Cut the mushrooms in half. Melt 1 oz. (2T) of the butter in a small frying pan and cook mushrooms gently until tender. Drain well. Melt the remaining 1 oz. (2T) butter in a saucepan, add flour and cook, stirring constantly until 'honeycombed' in appearance but not browned, 2–3 minutes. Add the reserved cooking liquor (liquid), bring to the boil, stirring, and simmer 3–4 minutes. Add the egg yolk, lemon juice, seasonings, mushrooms and mussels. Reheat without boiling.

Arrange fillets in a heated serving dish and pour the sauce over. Garnish with watercress.

Sole Normandy-style   serves 4

Sole niçoise — Fillets of sole Nice-style

2×12 oz. lemon or Dover sole
salt and freshly ground
black pepper
lemon juice
3 tablespoons (¼ cup) béchamel
sauce (see recipe page 16)
¼ teaspoon cayenne pepper
½ pint (1¼ cups) court bouillon
(see recipe page 30)
1 pint (2½ cups) sauce de tomates
Provençale (see recipe page 20)
chopped gherkin and 4 pitted
black olives for garnish

serves 4

Skin the soles and fillet. Cut each fillet in half down the centre and trim.

Season each fillet with salt, freshly ground black pepper and a little lemon juice. Chop the trimmings and mix with the sauce béchamel and cayenne pepper. Spread an eighth of the sauce mixture on each fillet and roll up from head to tail, keeping the cut side straight. Place the paupiettes (cut side downwards) in an ovenproof dish with the court bouillon. Cover and bake in a moderate oven (350°F. Mark 4) for 20 minutes.

Drain the fish, place it on a heated serving dish. Have the tomato sauce piping hot and coat the sole with it. Garnish with chopped gherkin and place half a black olive on each paupiette. Serve as soon as possible.

note: use plaice or flounder if sole is not available.

Truites amandines
Trout with almonds

4 trout
salt and pepper
4 oz. (8T) clarified butter
2 oz. (½ cup) blanched almonds

This dish is at its best when eaten in the Grenoble area. Here there is an abundance of rivers coming down from the Alps and the river trout are delicious, especially when freshly caught.

Wipe the trout, but do not remove the heads. Sprinkle with salt and pepper.
Heat the clarified butter in a large frying pan and fry the trout until cooked and golden, about 10–15 minutes. Drain the fish and place on a heated serving dish.
Slice the almonds into shreds and fry in butter in the pan until browned. Pour the butter and almonds over the trout and serve immediately.

serves 4

Truite saumonée en aspic
Salmon trout in aspic

1 × 3–4 lb. salmon trout
1½–2 pints (3¾–5 cups) court bouillon (see recipe page 30)
2 pints (5 cups) fish stock (see recipe page 30)
2 egg whites
2 oz. gelatine
3 tablespoons (¼ cup) sherry
prawns (shrimp), cucumber and lemon for garnish
mayonnaise for serving

Wash the trout, clean the cavities and rub with salt, then rinse. Curl the trout and place it in a deep ovenproof dish. Add the court bouillon and cover with a lid or aluminium foil, making sure it does not touch the fish. Bake in a moderately slow oven (325°F. Mark 3) for 40–50 minutes, basting frequently. Cool in the cooking liquid. Remove the skin. Make a cut on either side of the back bone, snip at each end and remove the back bone carefully. Place the fish stock in a large saucepan; an enamel or tin lined pan is best. Add egg whites and gelatine and whisk with a wire or balloon whisk. Bring slowly to the boil, whisking constantly. Remove from the heat and leave for 20 minutes. Strain through a scalded jelly bag or cloth. Stir in sherry and allow to cool.
Spoon the aspic carefully over the cooked salmon trout until it is glazed with a thin layer of jelly. Pour a thin layer of jelly in the base of a serving plate; allow to set. Very carefully lift the fish on to the serving dish. Garnish with chopped aspic, prawns (shrimp), cucumber and lemon slices. Serve the mayonnaise separately.

note: salmon may be prepared in the same way, but frequently they are too large and can only be served in individual steaks. It is sometimes easier to lift the fish on to the serving dish with the back bone still intact. Remove it when the salmon trout is actually on the dish.

serves 6

Mayonnaise de poisson
Fish mayonnaise

1 small lettuce
sauce vinaigrette (see recipe page 21)
1 lb. cooked white fish or shellfish
½ pint (1¼ cups) home made mayonnaise (see recipe page 20)
6 anchovy fillets
milk
capers
6 stuffed olives
1 tomato, skinned and sliced
1 hard-boiled egg, sliced

serves 4

Wash the lettuce, dry it and cut it into thin shreds. Toss the lettuce in a little sauce vinaigrette and drain again. Remove all skin and bones from the fish; flake.
Arrange the lettuce in a serving dish and place the cooked fish on top. Coat the fish evenly with home made mayonnaise. Soak the anchovies in milk for 20 minutes, drain. Garnish the home made mayonnaise with strips of anchovy fillet arranged in a trellis with a caper in each space. Place halved stuffed olives, tomato slices and hard-boiled egg around the edge.
Serve as soon as possible.

Coquilles St. Jacques à la breton
Scallops Breton-style

1 lb. Mediterranean, Pacific or Atlantic scallops
4 oz. (8T) melted butter
8 tablespoons (¾ cup) fine browned breadcrumbs
½ clove garlic, well crushed
1 teaspoon finely chopped parsley
salt and freshly ground black pepper

serves 4

Scallops are readily available (when in season) in nearly all parts of the world. There are many ways of serving them but this extremely simple recipe is one of the best ways. Scallops also vary in size so although 2–3 scallops will be more than enough for one person when they come from the Atlantic, you will need 4–5 Pacific or Mediterranean scallops for each serving.
Trim the scallops and remove the strip of skin and muscle on the outside. Rinse, drain and slice the scallops into thick pieces. Grease 4 scallop shells or small ovenproof dishes with a little of the melted butter. Sprinkle with half the breadcrumbs. Divide the sliced scallops equally between the four shells.
Mix the remaining breadcrumbs with the garlic and parsley, season. Cover the scallops with the breadcrumb mixture and pour the remaining melted butter over the top. Bake, uncovered, in a moderately slow oven (325°F. Mark 3) for 15–20 minutes. Serve in the shells.

Crab garni
Dressed crab

1 medium sized crab, cooked
2 tablespoons (2½T) browned breadcrumbs
salt, pepper and dry mustard
2 hard-boiled egg yolks, chopped or grated

serves 2–4

Remove the small claws and reserve. Remove the large claws, crack them open and remove all the flesh. Separate the upper and lower parts of the crab shell by pulling them apart, holding them with a clean tea towel. Remove the small sac on top of the big shell near the head, the spongy gills and any green matter in the big shell. Scrape out the brown creamy meat which lies around the sides of the big shell. Mix it with browned breadcrumbs, salt, pepper and mustard Break the crab body in half and remove all the white meat carefully. Use a skewer and be careful not to break off any shell. Mix all the white meat together and chop. Season.
Scrub the main body shell, rinse and dry thoroughly. Arrange the crab meat in the shell in rows with the egg yolk. Put a wide band of dark meat down the centre, egg yolk on either side and then two rows of white meat, one each side.
Serve as soon as possible. Serve a salad, home made mayonnaise and thin slices of brown bread and butter, separately.

note: if you are fortunate enough to have a freshly caught crab, first kill it by plunging it into boiling water. Cook it in court bouillon (see recipe page 30) allowing 15 minutes for each lb. weight.

Dressed crab

Bouillabaisse   Provençale fish stew

2–3 lb. fish *Use a mixture of at least 5 varieties: John Dory, whiting, turbot, bass, mullet, conger eel, hake, halibut, cod, lobster and red or grey snapper are all suitable. Also include some langoustine or king prawns (shrimp)*
3 tablespoons (¼ cup) olive oil
1 onion, chopped
3 red tomatoes, skinned, deseeded and chopped
2 cloves garlic, crushed
bouquet garni
salt and pepper
pinch of saffron
2 pints (5 cups) water, boiling
¼ pint (⅝ cup) white wine, optional
8 slices French bread
2 tablespoons (2½T) finely chopped parsley
serves 6–8

Bouillabaisse can really only be made properly with fish and shellfish which come only from the Mediterranean Sea. It is possible, however, to make a very good imitation with fish that are available elsewhere.

Wash the fish, removing all the bones and any skin. Cut into thick slices (but not the prawns [shrimp]).
Heat the olive oil in a large saucepan, add the onion and cook until softened, stirring constantly. Add the tomatoes, garlic and bouquet garni. Season, then add the saffron and the boiling water. Add the firm-fleshed fish (not the prawns [shrimp], John Dory or whiting). Bring to the boil again and cook rapidly, uncovered, for 10 minutes. Add the prawns (shrimps), soft fish and wine. Continue cooking for another 5 minutes. Shake the pan occasionally to prevent the fish from sticking.
Place the slices of bread in a deep, heated serving dish, pour the cooking liquid in and make sure that it is all absorbed. Arrange the fish, according to variety, on the bread. Serve immediately, sprinkled with chopped parsley.

note: the bread may be served separately if liked.

Prawn butter balls

Provençale fish stew

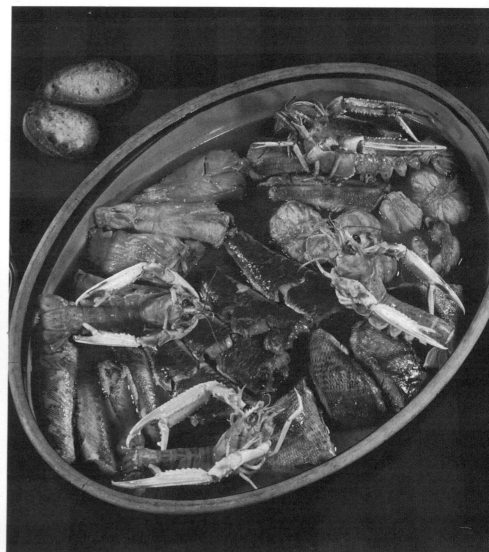

Trout with almonds

Homard thermidor — Lobster thermidor

2×12 oz. lobsters
1 oz. (2T) butter
½ teaspoon each dried chervil,
tarragon and parsley
1 shallot, chopped
¼ pint (⅝ cup) white wine
¼ pint (⅝ cup) double (heavy) cream
¼ pint (⅝ cup) sauce béchamel
(see recipe page 16)
¼ pint (⅝ cup) fish stock (see
recipe page 30)
¼ teaspoon paprika pepper
½ teaspoon dry mustard
salt
3 oz. (¾ cup) grated
Parmesan cheese
serves 4

Split the lobsters in half lengthwise, removing all the meat from the shells and from the claws. Chop roughly.
Melt the butter in a saucepan, then add the herbs and shallot and cook for 1 minute. Add the wine and simmer 5 minutes. Add the cream and sauce béchamel, bring to the boil and simmer until thick and creamy. Add the fish stock, reheat, season with paprika pepper, mustard and salt. Stir in half of the cheese.
Mix the lobster meat with the hot sauce. Pile the meat back into the shell halves, sprinkle with remaining cheese and brown the tops under a hot grill.
Serve as soon as possible.

note: use fresh herbs if available; 1 teaspoon, chopped, of each herb is enough.

Moules marinière — Mussels in wine sauce

4 dozen mussels
¼ pint (⅝ cup) white wine
½ pint (1¼ cups) water
bouquet garni
1 carrot, thinly sliced
2 shallots, chopped
1 clove garlic, crushed
6 black peppercorns
salt to taste
1 tablespoon (1¼T)
chopped parsley
3 tablespoons (¼ cup) single
(light) cream
2 egg yolks

serves 4

Wash the mussels, remove weed and discard any that have opened. Place them in a large saucepan with the wine, water, carrot, shallots, garlic and peppercorns. Bring to the boil, slowly, then simmer for 5 minutes, shaking the pan gently until all the shells have opened. Arrange the mussels in a serving dish and keep them warm. Strain the cooking liquid and return it to the saucepan. Bring to the boil and continue boiling rapidly until the liquid has reduced to a third of the quantity. Mix the cream with the egg yolks and add to the pan with the salt and parsley. Cook, without boiling, until slightly thickened.
Pour sauce over the mussels and serve immediately.

note: the egg yolks may be omitted. They can also be replaced by a beurre manié.
Cream ½ oz. (2T) flour with ½ oz. (1T) butter, add to the pan in small pieces, bring to the boil and cook 2–3 minutes. Only add enough beurre manié to obtain a creamy sauce. Add the cream afterwards; do not boil.

La bourride — Fish in garlic sauce

1½ lb. white fish (use 3 different kinds as available e.g. John Dory, turbot, bass)
1 fish head and bones
court bouillon (see recipe page 30)
½ pint (1¼ cups) sauce aïoli (see recipe page 21)
2 egg yolks
8 rounds toasted French bread for serving
chopped parsley for garnish

Although this is a Provençale dish, it can be easily reproduced using fish other than those caught only in the Mediterranean. The essential part of this recipe is the garlic sauce. Make sure that your guests like garlic before serving it to them!

Wash the fish, remove any bones and skin and cut it into thick slices. Place the fish head and bones in a saucepan with court bouillon. Bring to the boil and simmer for 10 minutes. Put the fish into a saucepan, add the strained court bouillon, to the depth of ½ inch, bring to the boil, cover and poach the fish gently for about 15 minutes or until just cooked. Drain, keep hot. Boil the stock in a pan until 3 tablespoons (3¾T) remain.
Place half of the prepared sauce aïoli in the top of a double boiler (or in a bowl) over hot water. Heat gently, add the egg yolks and cook, stirring, until it begins to thicken. Beat in the reduced fish stock. Put the drained fish in a heated serving dish, pour over the sauce. Serve with rounds of toasted French bread and garnished with chopped parsley. Serve the remaining sauce aïoli separately.

note: a piece of orange peel and a sprig of fennel can be added to the court bouillon, if available.

serves 4

Harengs breton
Herrings Brittany-style

3 oz. (6T) butter
4 dessert apples, cored
3 sticks celery, chopped
½ onion, grated
½ pint (1¼ cups) cider (hard)
salt and pepper
4 herrings, cleaned, with heads and fins removed
sprigs of parsley for garnish

serves 4

Melt 1 oz. (2T) of butter in a large frying pan. Chop 2 of the apples and add them to the pan with the celery and onion. Fry gently for 10 minutes. Add the (hard) cider, salt and pepper and simmer, uncovered, for a further 10 minutes. Place the cider mixture on a serving plate and keep hot.
Melt the remaining 2 oz. (4T) butter in cleaned pan. Slice the remaining apples and fry them for 3 minutes on each side. Remove from the pan and keep hot. Fry the prepared herrings in the same frying pan for 4–5 minutes on each side. Drain the cooked herrings and place on the cider mixture on the serving plate. Garnish with fried apple slices and sprigs of parsley.
Serve very hot.

Rougets provençales
Red mullet with garlic and herbs

4×12 oz. red mullet
salt
3 tablespoons (¼ cup) lemon juice
3 tablespoons (¼ cup) chopped parsley
1 clove garlic, crushed
1 oz. butter, softened
2 tablespoons French mustard
pinch of mixed dried herbs
extra lemon juice
serves 4

Clean the mullet, season, and place them in an oiled roasting pan. Sprinkle them with lemon juice and the parsley and garlic mixed together. Bake, uncovered, in a moderately hot oven (375°F. Mark 5) for 20 minutes.
Blend together the butter, mustard, herbs and a little extra lemon juice. Make it into a roll, wrap in greaseproof paper and chill, then slice into rounds.
Serve the mullet on a heated serving plate, topped with the herbed butter.

Huîtres
Oysters

Oysters are mainly found around the Normandy and Brittany coast. They are at their best when served raw.
Open them just before they are to be served. Serve the oyster in the deep half of the shell and stand the shells on a bed of crushed ice. Sprinkle each oyster with a little cayenne pepper and garnish with a lemon wedge. Serve thinly sliced brown bread and butter separately. Allow 6–12 oysters for each person.

Meat

Meat is expensive compared with other foods, and nowhere is this more true than in France. It is because of the price of meat that the French housewife buys it with such care and, in consequence, the French butchers have developed their own style of presenting their meat. All the excess fat and sinews are trimmed off so that the housewife can see exactly what she is buying. Joints are neatly tied, cutlets have the top inch of bone bare (Frenched) ready for a cutlet frill. Tournados steaks have a piece of bacon or a thin strip of fat tied around the outside, to keep them moist. If the cut of meat to be roasted is rather dry, such as topside or aitchbone, the butcher will 'lard' it by threading thin strips of fat into the meat with a special 'larding needle'. You can buy larding needles in this country or alternatively, simply bard the meat with rashers of fat bacon. Pork is the fattest of the meats and almost never has to be larded. It is pork fat that is most commonly used for larding beef and veal. Lamb cuts rarely need larding.

The cuts of meat used in France are not always available elsewhere. I have given the more familiar cuts which your butcher will understand. Buy them with care and cook them carefully following the recipe – you will achieve a truly French dish.

In the average French home, meat is not eaten every day, for economy reasons. If, however, it is served at a dinner party, you will frequently find that it appears twice on the menu, once as the entrée which is a made dish, and once as a joint to be carved at the table – this course is called the relevé. Naturally, a dinner such as this would be extremely formal and on most occasions meat would only be served at one course, either for the entrée or the relevé.

Some of the recipes in this chapter are ideal for family meals. Try your family with a pot-au-feu or côte d'agneau à la Bretonne; you will receive praise indeed!

Preparing meat

La daube de boeuf Provençale
Provençale beef stew

2 lb. stewing beef; chuck, round or blade are all suitable
½ pint (1¼ cups) red wine
3 tablespoons (¼ cup) olive oil
bouquet garni
thin strip orange peel
2 rashers streaky bacon, diced
2 carrots, sliced
2 onions, sliced
2 oz. button mushrooms
4 tomatoes, skinned, deseeded and chopped
2 cloves garlic, crushed
1 tablespoon chopped parsley
salt and freshly ground black pepper
½ pint (1¼ cups) fond brun (beef bone stock) (see recipe page 30)
12 black olives, pitted
serves 4–6

There are many different recipes for this dish. It must, however, include wine, herbs and garlic. The remaining ingredients (except the beef) may include whatever is available at the time. This is an old farmhouse recipe.

Cut the beef into large cubes and place in a bowl with the wine, olive oil, bouquet garni and orange peel. Marinate the beef for 3–4 hours.
Place the bacon in a flameproof casserole. Heat, and fry the bacon until softened, add the carrots, onions, mushrooms, tomatoes, garlic, parsley and seasonings. Stir, then cover the casserole and cook very gently for 5–10 minutes. Add the beef and the marinade, to the stock, bring to the boil, then cover the casserole tightly and place in a slow oven (275°F. Mark 1) for 2½–3 hours. Add the olives 30 minutes before cooking time is completed. Remove the bouquet garni and the orange peel.
Serve hot, in the casserole.

note: this dish is frequently served with noodles. Toss the cooked noodles with a little of the gravy before serving.

Boeuf bourguignonne
Beef cooked in Burgundy wine

2 lb. topside steak (rump pot roast)
4 oz. pickled pork
2 oz. (4T) butter
2 tablespoons (2½T) oil
12 very small onions or shallots
1 oz. (¼ cup) plain (all purpose) flour
¼ pint (⅝ cup) fond brun (beef bone stock, see recipe page 30)
2 cloves garlic, crushed
bouquet garni
salt and freshly ground black pepper
½ bottle (13 fluid oz.) red Burgundy wine
4 oz. button mushrooms
croûtes of fried bread
chopped parsley for garnish

serves 4–6

This dish is one of the great classics. It came originally from the Burgundy province in eastern France but is now cooked all over the country. Red Burgundy wine is still an essential ingredient.

Trim the meat, removing excess fat. Cut the beef into 2 inch cubes. Put the pork in a small saucepan, cover with water, bring to the boil and simmer for 5 minutes. Drain and slice the pork into thin strips.
Heat 1 oz. (2T) of the butter with the oil in a flameproof casserole. Add the peeled onions and fry gently until browned all over. Remove and drain. Add the beef and pork and fry until browned. Remove and drain. Add the flour to the casserole and cook, stirring constantly for 2–3 minutes. Add the stock, garlic, bouquet garni and seasonings, then return the meat to the casserole. Heat the wine in a small saucepan, ignite and pour over the beef.
Cover the casserole and cook in a slow oven (300°F. Mark 2) for 1½–2 hours.
Heat the remaining 1 oz. (2T) butter in a small frying pan and fry the mushrooms for 3–4 minutes. Add the mushrooms and onions to the casserole 30 minutes before cooking time is completed.
Serve hot, in the casserole, garnished with croûtes of bread and chopped parsley.

Boeuf à la mode
Beef à la mode

1 × 4 lb. piece top rump beef
2 oz. (¼ cup) dripping
½ pint (1¼ cups) red wine
fond brun (beef bone stock)
(see recipe page 30)
4 rashers streaky bacon
1 small calf's foot
3 carrots
3 onions
bouquet garni
salt and freshly ground
black pepper

Wipe the meat. Heat the dripping in a heavy, flameproof casserole and fry the beef until browned all over. Pour off excess fat. Add the wine, bring to the boil and simmer until the quantity of the wine is reduced by half. Add enough stock to almost cover the beef.
Cut the bacon into strips and place in a small saucepan with the calf's foot. Cover with cold water, bring to the boil and simmer for 4–5 minutes. Drain and rinse in cold water. Add the bacon, calf's foot, whole peeled vegetables, bouquet garni and salt and pepper to the casserole.
Cover the casserole tightly and cook in a very slow oven (275 °F. Mark 1) for 5 hours.
Place the meat on a serving dish, strain the gravy and pour it over. If the meat is to be served cold, place the beef in a bowl, pour over the strained gravy and allow it to become a jelly (jello).

serves 8–10

note: do not serve the cooking vegetables; by now, they will be very overcooked.

Pot-au-feu
Boiled beef and soup

3 lb. rolled rib of beef
1 lb. veal bones
½ tablespoon salt
2 carrots
2 leeks
2 onions
4 cloves
1 turnip
2 sticks celery
bouquet garni
freshly ground black pepper

This classic French dish is the basis of an excellent soup, or can serve as a strong stock for use in soups (with additional ingredients) or even for consommé. The beef is served as a separate course, accompanied by the vegetables.
Place the beef in a large saucepan with the veal bones and salt. Add 6 pints (15 cups) of water. Bring slowly to the boil and remove the scum with a metal spoon. Skim again as necessary. Simmer gently for 30 minutes.
Prepare the vegetables, cutting them in half or quarters if large, otherwise leaving them whole. Stick the cloves into one of the onions. Add the vegetables to the pan with the bouquet garni and some freshly ground black pepper. Continue cooking for a further 2–2½ hours or until the meat is tender.
Serve the beef on a heated dish, surrounded by the vegetables. Return the soup to the heat and continue cooking for a further 1 hour. Use as required.

serves 4–6

note: originally, pot-au-feu was simply a stockpot. Today it is considered too wasteful to use 3 lb. beef only for stock so it is removed when tender and not left in the pan for the complete cooking time.

Chateaubriand

A chateaubriand steak is also cut from the middle of the fillet. It usually weighs 1 lb. or more and is almost a small joint. It is always grilled, however, and this must be done very carefully so that the outside does not become over-brown before the middle is cooked.
First seal the outside quickly under a very hot grill, then reduce the temperature and continue cooking for about 20 minutes, (or until cooked to your liking). Baste the steak occasionally with melted butter. Serve the chateaubriand with maître d'hôtel butter (see recipe page 51) or sauce béarnaise (see recipe page 18).
Chateaubriand originally got its name from the château potatoes which are the traditional accompaniment. The recipe for these is on page 88.

serves 2–3

Fillet steaks béarnaise (above)

Loin of lamb with haricot beans (right)

Beef cooked in burgundy wine (far right)

Tournedos de boeuf   Fillet steaks

4 × 4–6 oz. tournedos steaks
salt and freshly ground
black pepper
2 oz. (4T) clarified butter
4 croûtes fried bread

The middle of the fillet, when cut into a 1½–2 inch slice, is called a tournados. It is the most tender piece of the whole animal and should be cooked with extreme care. Try cooking it at the table, pouring 2 tablespoons (2½T) of warmed brandy over the top and igniting.
Serve when the flames die down.

Trim the steaks, removing the skin from around the edge. Cut away the majority of the fat. Sprinkle each steak with salt and freshly ground black pepper.
Heat the butter in a large heavy frying pan, add the prepared steaks and cook for 3–4 minutes on each side, turning once. This cooking time will give a rare to medium-rare steak; allow a little more time for frying each side for a medium or well-done steak, if preferred.

serves 4

Serve each steak on a fried croûte of bread.

Tournedos à la pompadour

Pour a little of the butter in the frying pan over the steaks, place a slice of grilled tomato on top and a small piece of maître d'hôtel butter (see recipe page 51) on top of this.

Tournados à la béarnaise

Place 2 teaspoons of sauce béarnaise (see recipe page 18) on each steak. Garnish with sprigs of watercress.

Tournedos chasseur

Place 2 teaspoons of sauce chasseur (see recipe page 16) on top of each steak. Garnish with a little chopped parsley.

Tournedos provençale

Omit the fried croûtes of bread and use instead ¼–½ inch slices of aubergine. Sprinkle them with salt, leave for 30 minutes, rinse and drain well. Fry in butter until golden. Top each steak with a little sauce de tomate provençale (see recipe page 20).

Tournedos au poivre

Crush 1 tablespoon (1¼T) whole peppercorns (black or white) with a rolling pin. (It is easiest if you put the peppercorns between two pieces of greaseproof paper.) Press the crushed peppercorns into the tournados on both sides, before cooking. Cook in the usual way. Serve the tournados on croûtes. Add 1 tablespoon (1¼T) brandy to the juices in the pan, ignite, and pour the flaming brandy over the top.

Tournedos jardinière

Serve the steaks on a bed of freshly cooked mixed vegetables. Use new potatoes, carrots, peppers and peas. Cook them individually and toss together with a little melted butter and seasonings.

Filet de boeuf dubarry
Roast beef fillet with cheese and cauliflower

1 × 3 lb. fillet of beef
2 oz. (4T) butter
4 rashers streaky bacon
freshly ground black pepper
1 cauliflower
1 pint (2½ cups) sauce mornay
(see recipe page 17)
2 oz. (½ cup) grated
Parmesan cheese
parsley for garnish

This recipe was reputedly a favourite of Madame Dubarry, a famous courtesan at the court of King Louis XIV.

Trim the excess fat from the fillet. Heat the butter in a roasting pan, place the fillet in the pan and lay the rashers of bacon on top. Baste with the butter and sprinkle with freshly ground black pepper. Roast in a hot oven (425°F. Mark 7) for 30–40 minutes or until the fillet is cooked medium-rare. (If you like well cooked meat, extend the cooking time accordingly.)
Meanwhile, cut the cauliflower into florets. Cook the cauliflower in a saucepan of boiling salted water for 10 minutes or until tender. Place the cauliflower around the fillet on a heated serving plate and coat with sauce mornay. Sprinkle the top with Parmesan cheese and place under a hot grill until golden. Garnish with sprigs of parsley and serve immediately.

serves 6

Filet de boeuf en croûte
Fillet of beef in pastry

1 × 3 lb. fillet of beef
salt and freshly ground
black pepper
2 oz. (4T) butter
8 oz. pâte feuilletée. (see recipe
page 119)
1 egg yolk

Rub the fillet with salt and pepper. Melt the butter in a frying pan and fry the fillet until browned all over. Use a pair of tongs or 2 spoons to turn it so as not to pierce the outside. Remove and cool. Roll out the pastry on a lightly floured surface to ⅛ inch thick and large enough to enclose the whole fillet. Trim the pastry and place the beef in the centre. Fold the pastry around the meat, brush a little egg yolk along the edges and seal the pastry around the meat. Cut pastry leaves from the trimmings and stick them on to the top of the pastry with egg yolk. Brush the pastry and leaves all over with egg yolk.
Bake in a very hot oven (450°F. Mark 8) for 15 minutes. Reduce the heat to moderate (350°F. Mark 4) for a further 15–20 minutes. Serve as soon as possible.

note: the meat will be rare. If you like your meat medium or well-done, extend the cooking time accordingly.

serves 6–8

Alouettes sans Têtes
Stuffed beef rolls

1 lb. topside (round) steak
1 onion, sliced
1 carrot, sliced
1 stick celery, sliced
2 rashers streaky bacon, chopped
salt and black pepper
¼ pint (⅝ cup) red wine
½ pint (1¼ cups) fond brun
(beef bone stock see page 30)
· 1 teaspoon tomato paste
bouquet garni
choppped parsley for garnish

stuffing:
1 oz. (¼ cup) finely chopped ham
1 clove garlic, crushed
2 teaspoons chopped parsley
3 tablespoons (¼ cup) breadcrumbs
1 teaspoon grated lemon rind
salt and pepper
pinch of ground nutmeg
milk

serves 4–6

Literally, 'alouettes sans têtes' means 'larks without heads'!

Slice the beef into very thin slices, place each slice between 2 pieces of polythene and beat well with a rolling pin until wafer thin.
Cut the slices into pieces about 2 inches by 4 inches.
Mix all the stuffing ingredients together, adding sufficient milk to bind. Place a teaspoon of the stuffing on each piece of beef, roll up and tie with thread.
Place the onion, carrot and celery with the bacon in the base of an ovenproof dish. Put the 'alouettes' on top and season with salt and pepper. Pour in the wine and the stock, mixed with the tomato paste and add the bouquet garni.
Cover the dish with greased greaseproof paper and cook in a moderately slow oven (325°F. Mark 3) for about 2 hours, or until very tender. Remove the 'alouettes', then untie and discard the cotton. Strain the gravy into a saucepan, reheat and add the 'alouettes' to the pan. Simmer 2–3 minutes.
Serve in a heated dish, sprinkled with chopped parsley.

Le fricandeau   Braised veal

1½ lb. veal
4 rashers streaky bacon
4 oz. pickled pork, diced
1 large onion, sliced
1 large carrot, sliced
¼ pint (⅝ cup) white wine
1 pint (2½ cups) fond blanc
(white stock) see recipe
page 30)
bouquet garni
salt and pepper
chopped parsley for garnish

Le fricandeau is a long sliver of veal which is cut from under the
'nut' of veal which is the top of the leg. It is usually about 1½ inches
thick and is cut along the grain of the meat. This recipe is the
classic for cooking 'le fricandeau'.

Cut the veal into 1½ inch slices (see above). Cut the bacon into
long strips. Place the pickled pork in the base of a large, heavy,
flameproof casserole, add the vegetables and then the veal and cover
with the bacon. Heat the casserole very gently, cover and cook for
20–25 minutes. Add the wine, cover, and cook for 15–20 minutes.
Add ¼ pint (⅝ cup) of the stock, cover and cook for 15–20 minutes
or until the liquid is well reduced. Add another ¼ pint (⅝ cup) of
stock and cook as before. Pour in the remaining stock, cover the
casserole tightly and cook in a moderately slow oven (325 °F. Mark 3)
for 1½ hours.
Remove the meat and strain the gravy. Place the meat in a saucepan,
pour over the gravy, adjust seasonings and cook rapidly, turning
the meat over occasionally, until the liquid is reduced to ¼–½ pint
(⅝–1¼ cups).
Serve the meat with the thickened gravy poured over it. Garnish
with chopped parsley.

note: at no time should this dish be allowed to brown. The veal
should be extremely tender when cooked and the gravy should give
a good glaze.

serves 4

Escalopes de veau à la savoyard
Veal escalopes with cream sauce

4×4–4½ oz. veal escalopes
salt and pepper
lemon juice
2 oz. (4T) butter
6 tablespoons (½ cup) dry
white vermouth
6 tablespoons (½ cup) double
(heavy) cream
4 slices of lemon for garnish

This delicious recipe comes from the Alpine Savoie department of France. Savoie is famed for its dairy produce and the capital town of Chambery is also known for the locally produced dry white vermouth.

Trim the escalopes and place them between two sheets of polythene. Using a small mallet or a rolling pin, beat the veal until it is about ⅛ inch thick. Season with salt, pepper and lemon juice.
Melt the butter in a very large frying pan until very hot, add the escalopes and fry until they are beginning to brown, turning once. Add the vermouth and bring to the boil. Add the cream and continue cooking, shaking the pan occasionally, until the vermouth and cream are combined and thickened.
Serve on a heated serving dish, garnished with slices of lemon.

note: if your frying pan is not large enough to take the 4 escalopes all at once, fry them 2 at a time and return the first to the pan just before adding the vermouth.

serves 4

Blanquette de veau
Veal stew

1½ lb. stewing veal
10 small onions or shallots
2 oz. (4T) butter
2 oz. (½ cup) plain (all
purpose) flour
1½ pints (3¾ cups) fond blanc
(white stock) see recipe page 30)
bouquet garni
6 white peppercorns
4 oz. mushrooms
2 teaspoons lemon juice
¼ pint (⅝ cup) single
(light) cream
salt
croûtes of fried bread
small grilled bacon rolls (rashers
of bacon rolled up and secured
with a tooth pick)
chopped parsley

serves 4

Trim the meat and cut it into 2 inch cubes. Peel the onions. Heat the butter in a saucepan, add the meat and fry until it has changed colour, but do not allow it to brown. Remove and drain the meat, add the onions and fry for 4–5 minutes, without browning.
Remove and drain. Stir the flour into the saucepan and cook gently, stirring constantly, until the roux is 'honeycombed' in appearance but has not browned, 3–4 minutes.
Add stock and heat, stirring, until boiling. Add the bouquet garni, peppercorns and the washed stalks from the mushrooms. Simmer for 20 minutes.
Strain the gravy into a clean saucepan, add the veal and onions, cover, and continue cooking for 1–1½ hours or until meat is tender. Add the chopped mushrooms (or whole button mushrooms) 15 minutes before cooking time is finished. Add the lemon juice and cream, taste and adjust the seasoning.
Reheat without boiling.
Serve in a heated dish garnished with croûtes of bread, bacon rolls and chopped parsley.

Stuffed ham rolls (right)

Provençale beef stew (far right)

Longe de veau rôti   Roast loin of veal

1 × 3 lb. loin of veal, boned
salt and pepper
1 teaspoon dried
rosemary chopped
4 rashers streaky bacon
3 tablespoons (¼ cup) olive oil
serves 4

Rub the veal all over with salt and pepper. Tie it firmly in a roll.
Place the meat in a roasting pan, sprinkle with rosemary and place
the bacon over the top. Roast in a moderate oven (350°F. Mark 4) for
2 hours (allowing 40 minutes for each lb.). Baste with oil every
20 minutes.
Serve sliced on a heated serving dish.

Gigot d'agneau en croûte   Roast leg of lamb in pastry case

1 × 4 lb. leg of lamb, boned
4 lambs' kidneys
3 oz. (6T) butter
1 clove garlic, crushed
salt and pepper
8 oz. pâte feuilletée (see recipe
page 119)
1 egg yolk

Wipe the leg of lamb and trim off the excess fat. Skin the kidneys,
cut in half and remove the tubes. Melt 1 oz. (2T) of the butter in a
frying pan and fry the kidney with the garlic until tender, 3–4
minutes. Season with salt and pepper and place the kidney mixture
into the cavity. Tie securely with fine string. Place in a roasting pan,
rub with the remaining 2 oz. (4T) butter and roast in a hot oven
(425°F. Mark 7) for 1 hour (allowing 15 minutes cooking time for
each lb.). Remove and allow to cool.
Roll out the prepared pastry to a size which will envelop the leg of
lamb. Place the lamb on the pastry, moisten the edges and wrap the
meat up firmly, pressing the edges together. Brush the pastry with
the egg yolk. Bake in a hot oven (as before) for 15–20 minutes, or
until golden and crisp.

serves 6   Serve, ready for carving, on a heated plate.

Navarin d'agneau   Lamb stew

1½ lb. lean lamb, shoulder or
middle neck
3 tablespoons (¼ cup) oil
4 onions
4 carrots
1 turnip
1 oz. (¼ cup) plain (all
purpose) flour
1 pint (2½ cups) fond blanc
(white stock, see recipe page 30)
bouquet garni
1 tablespoon tomato paste
1 clove garlic, crushed
salt and pepper
parsley for garnish
serves 4

Trim the meat and cut it into 1 inch cubes. Heat the oil in a large
heavy saucepan and fry the meat until it has changed colour. Peel
and slice the onions, peel and dice the carrots and turnip. Add the
vegetables to the saucepan and fry until beginning to brown. Stir in
the flour and cook, stirring constantly for 3–4 minutes.
Return the lamb to the saucepan, add the stock, bouquet garni,
tomato paste, garlic, salt and pepper. Cover the saucepan. Bring to
the boil and simmer very gently for 1½–2 hours or until the meat is
very tender. Serve in a heated dish, garnished with sprigs of parsley.

note: if mutton is used, adjust the cooking time to 2–2½ hours, or
until the meat is very tender.

Noisettes d'agneau béarnaise   Noisettes of lamb with béarnaise sauce

2 lb. best end of neck
salt and pepper
½ teaspoon dried basil
½ pint (1¼ cups) sauce béarnaise
(see recipe page 18)
croûtes of fried bread

Ask the butcher to chine the meat. Remove the chine bone, rib bones
and the skin. Sprinkle the meat with salt, pepper and basil. Roll the
meat up tightly, starting with the thick side. Tie the meat securely
in 1½ inch lengths and slice into noisettes.
Grill the noisettes under a hot grill, turning once, until the meat is
sealed. Reduce the heat of the grill and continue cooking for 5–10
minutes or until the lamb is just cooked.
Serve each noisette on a croûte of bread. Top with a spoonful of
sauce béarnaise. Place on a heated dish and serve immediately.

serves 4   **note:** noisettes can also be prepared and served as for lamb cutlets.

Lamb cutlets

Côtelettes d'agneau soubise
Lamb cutlets with onions

8 lamb cutlets, from the best end of neck
1 oz. (2T) butter
1 small onion, sliced
salt and pepper
bay leaf
¼ pint (⅝ cup) white wine
¾ pint (approx. 2 cups) sauce soubise (see recipe page 17)
fried onion rings for garnish (see recipe page 93)
serves 4

Trim the cutlets. Heat the butter in a large saucepan, add the cutlets and brown all over. Remove the cutlets, add the onion and fry until golden. Return the cutlets to the saucepan and add salt, pepper, a bay leaf and white wine. Cover the pan and simmer very gently for 15–20 minutes.
Serve the cutlets on a heated serving plate, coat in sauce soubise and garnish with fried onion rings.

Côtelettes d'agneau provençale

Omit the sauce soubise and the fried onions from the above recipe. Use instead ¾ pint (approx. 2 cups) sauce de tomate provençale (see recipe page 20).

Côtelettes d'agneau savoyard

Omit the sauce soubise and the fried onions from the above recipe. Use instead ¾ pint (approx. 2 cups) sauce mornay (see recipe page 17) and garnish with 4 oz. mushrooms, sliced and fried gently in 1 oz. (2T) butter.

Côte d'agneau à la bretonne
Loin of lamb with haricot beans

8 oz. dried haricot beans, soaked overnight
1 carrot
1 onion
bouquet garni
1 × 2 lb. loin of lamb, boned
salt
1 clove garlic
½ pint (1¼ cups) fond brun (beef bone stock, see recipe page 30)
2 large red tomatoes, skinned, deseeded and chopped

Brittany is renowned for producing delicious lamb. There are large expanses of salt meadows where lambs are pastured and it is these that give the meat its distinctive flavour.

Place the beans in a large saucepan with salted cold water to cover. Add the carrot, onion and bouquet garni. Bring to the boil and simmer for 2 hours or until tender.
Meanwhile, wipe the lamb, rub it all over with salt and insert slivers of garlic in various places just under the skin. Roll and tie with fine string.
Place the lamb in a greased roasting pan with the stock, cover with greased greaseproof paper and roast in a moderately hot oven (375°F. Mark 5) for 50 minutes. After 20 minutes remove the paper and baste with the stock in the pan; baste 2–3 more times during cooking and remove the paper completely for the last 10 minutes to allow the lamb to brown.
Place the meat on a heated serving plate and keep hot. Drain the cooked beans, remove and chop the onion and carrot. Mix the beans with the tomato, carrot and onion and a little of the meat stock, to moisten.
serves 4 Spoon the beans around the lamb and serve.

Côte de porc normande
Pork chops in cider

1 oz. (2T) butter
2 teaspoons oil
4 oz. button onions, peeled
4 pork chops
8 oz. tomatoes, skinned and quartered
2 sticks celery, cut into 1 inch lengths
2 dessert apples, cored and sliced
4 oz. button mushrooms, washed
¾ oz. (3 tablespoons) plain (all purpose flour)
¾ pint (scant 2 cups) fond blanc (white stock, see recipe page 30)
4 tablespoons (good ¼ cup) still cider (hard)
1 tablespoon dried thyme
salt and freshly ground black pepper
chopped parsley for garnish

serves 4

Heat the butter and oil together in a flameproof casserole. Add the onions and fry gently until golden brown. Add the pork chops and fry until browned on both sides. Mix the remaining vegetables and apple slices, add to the casserole and cook, stirring, for 3 minutes. Stir in the flour, cook 2–3 minutes. Pour in the stock and (hard) cider, add the thyme and season to taste.

Cover the casserole tightly and cook in a moderate oven (350°F. Mark 4) for 45 minutes.

Serve garnished with chopped parsley.

Carré de porc provençale
Loin of pork with garlic and herbs

1 × 3 lb. loin of pork
1 clove garlic
salt and pepper
½ teaspoon chopped dried thyme
¼ pint (⅝ cup) red wine
3 tablespoons (¼ cup) soft white breadcrumbs
3 tablespoons (¼ cup) finely chopped parsley

serves 4—6

Ask your butcher to chine the loin of pork. Cut off the skin but leave the fat unless it is very thick. Cut the garlic into thin slivers and insert them in various places, close to the bone. Rub salt and pepper into the pork then place it in a dish with the thyme and red wine. Marinate the meat for 2–3 hours.

Place the pork and the marinade in a roasting pan, fat side up. Cover with greased greaseproof paper or aluminium foil and roast in a moderate oven (350°F. Mark 4) for 1¼ hours. Remove the paper, mix the breadcrumbs and parsley together and press on to the pork fat with a palette knife. Baste with the cooking liquid and continue cooking in a slow oven (300°F. Mark 2) for 45 minutes. Baste occasionally.

Serve on a heated plate ready for carving into chops.

note: traditionally, this dish is served with pommes mousseline (see recipe page 88).

Pork chops in cider (left)   Cold meat and relishes (below)

Rôti de porc à la boulangère
Roast pork with sliced potatoes and apples

2 lb. boned and tied hand of
pork (boneless pork joint)
1½ lb. medium sized potatoes
3 apples
2 oz. (4T) butter
1 teaspoon dried
rosemary, chopped
salt and black pepper
serves 4–6

Wipe the meat and trim if necessary. Peel and slice the potatoes into
¼–½ inch slices. Peel and thinly slice the apples.
Cut the butter in small pieces and scatter them over the base of a
shallow roasting pan. Put apple slices on top of the potatoes,
overlapping in lines. Top with pork and sprinkle with rosemary and
salt and pepper. Roast in a hot oven (400°F. Mark 6) for 1 hour
(allowing 30 minutes cooking time for each lb.). Baste frequently.
Serve in the roasting pan in which it is cooked.

Jambon à la bourguignonne
Ham in red Burgundy wine

1 × 3 lb. gammon ham
1 onion
4 cloves
4 peppercorns
bouquet garni
1 carrot
½ bottle (13 fl. oz.) red Burgundy
½ tablespoon arrowroot

serves 6–8

Soak the ham overnight, if necessary, in cold water to cover. Next
day, drain and place it in a large saucepan, cover with fresh water
and add the onion, stuck with cloves, the peppercorns, bouquet garni
and carrot. Bring slowly to the boil and simmer for 1 hour.
Drain the ham and remove the skin. Place in an ovenproof casserole
with red wine and 1 pint (2½ cups) of the cooking liquid. Roast in a
moderately slow oven (325°F. Mark 3) for 1 hour, basting
occasionally. Remove the ham and strain the gravy into a saucepan.
Mix the arrowroot with a little water and add to the saucepan. Bring
to the boil, stirring constantly, and simmer 2–3 minutes.
Carve the ham into slices, arrange on a serving plate and pour over
the gravy.

Paupiettes de jambon
Stuffed ham rolls

8 slices cooked ham
2 sticks celery
2 apples
2 oz. (¾ cup) walnuts
1 tablespoon (1¼T)
chopped chives
1 tablespoon (1¼T) lemon juice
¼ pint (⅝ cup) home made
mayonnaise (see recipe page 20)
salt and pepper
4 oz. terrine de campagne (see
recipe page 28)
serves 4

Cut ham slices thinly and as large as possible. Chop the celery, peel,
core and chop the apples, chop the walnuts. Mix all these together
with the chives and lemon juice. Add home made mayonnaise, taste
and adjust the seasoning.
Spread each slice of ham with pâté. Divide the home made mayonnaise
mixture between the slices and roll up.
Serve the paupiettes on a bed of salad or garnished with parsley and
lemon slices.

Foie d'agneau farci
Stuffed lamb's liver

1 lb. lamb's liver
6 tablespoons (½ cup) white
breadcrumbs
1 oz. (2T) butter, melted
2 teaspoons chopped parsley
1 teaspoon grated lemon rind
½ teaspoon mixed dried herbs
1 shallot, finely chopped
salt and freshly ground
black pepper
¾ pint (approx. 2 cups) fond
brun (beef bone stock, see recipe
page 30)
4 rashers streaky bacon
serves 4

Wash, trim and slice the liver into ½–¾ inch slices. Arrange the slices
in an ovenproof serving dish.
Mix the breadcrumbs with butter, parsley, lemon rind, herbs,
chopped shallot and the seasonings. Divide into 4 and pack in 4
separate piles on top of the liver.
Pour the stock around the liver. Remove the rind from the bacon and
place on top of the stuffing. Cover with greased greaseproof paper or
aluminium foil and bake in a moderately hot oven (375°F. Mark 5)
for 1 hour. Remove the paper 15 minutes before cooking time is
completed to crisp the bacon.
Serve hot.

Foie de veau en brochette
Calves' liver kebabs

1½ lb. calves' liver
4 rashers bacon
4 small tomatoes, skinned
salt and black pepper
juice of ½ a lemon
1 teaspoon chopped dried basil
or marjoram
olive oil

serves 4

Wash the liver, trim and cut it into 1 inch cubes. Remove the rind from the bacon and cut into 1 inch pieces. Slice each tomato into 4. On each of 4 long skewers, thread first a piece of liver, then bacon and finally tomato. Continue until all the ingredients have been used. Sprinkle each brochette with salt, pepper, lemon juice, basil and oil. Cook under a moderately hot grill for 7–10 minutes, turning once. Serve on a heated plate.

note: this is delicious when served on ratatouille (see recipe page 93).

Rognons sauté turbigo
Fried kidneys with mushrooms and sausages

8 lamb's kidneys
1 oz. (2T) butter
4 oz. button mushrooms
12 small onions or shallots
4 thin pork sausages
½ pint (1¼ cups) sauce espagnole
(see recipe page 16)
salt and black pepper
croûtes of fried bread
chopped parsley for garnish

serves 4

Cut the kidneys in half lengthwise, cutting out the tubes and skin. Heat the butter in a saucepan, fry the mushrooms until tender, 2–3 minutes, remove and drain. Add the onions and fry them until browned all over, then remove. Cut the sausages into 1 inch lengths and fry, with the prepared kidneys, until browned. Return the onions to the saucepan and add the sauce espagnole. Cover the saucepan and simmer very gently for 15 minutes, stirring occasionally. Add the mushrooms and continue cooking for 5 minutes.
Serve in a heated dish, surrounded by croûtes of bread and sprinkled with chopped parsley.

Rognons de veau au vin blanc
Veal kidneys in white wine

4 small veal kidneys
1 oz. (2T) butter
1 tablespoon (1¼T) oil
1 onion, finely chopped
2 oz. mushrooms, sliced
½ pint (1¼ cups) fond brun
(beef bone stock see recipe
page 30)
¼ pint (⅝ cup) white wine
1 teaspoon tomato paste
salt and pepper
1 tablespoon (1¼T) arrowroot
chopped parsley for garnish

serves 4

Skin the kidneys and slice thinly. Heat the butter and oil in a saucepan and fry the kidneys until well browned, then remove them from the pan. Add the onion and fry until golden. Add the mushrooms and fry for a further 2–3 minutes. Pour in the stock and the wine, bring to the boil, add tomato paste and seasonings, then simmer for 5 minutes.
Add the fried kidneys. Mix the arrowroot with a little water and add to the pan, stirring. Bring to the boil, stirring constantly and simmer 2–3 minutes.
Serve in a heated dish, sprinkled with chopped parsley.

Ris de veau à la suprême
Sweetbreads in sauce velouté

1 lb. calves' sweetbreads
¾ pint (approx. 2 cups) sauce
velouté (see recipe page 19)
4 oz. button mushrooms
1 oz. (2T) butter
4 large croûtes of fried bread
chopped parsley for garnish

serves 4

Soak the sweetbreads in cold salted water for 1–2 hours. Bring a large saucepan of salted water to the boil, add the sweetbreads and cook for 3–4 minutes. Remove the sweetbreads from the pan and immerse in cold water to stop them cooking any further. Skin, then place them between two plates until cold.
Place in an ovenproof dish with ¼–½ inch depth of water. Cover with aluminium foil or greased greaseproof and cook in a moderate oven (350°F. Mark 4) for 20–25 minutes.
Prepare the sauce velouté. Fry the mushrooms in butter until cooked. Drain the sweetbreads and cut into ½ inch slices. Place them in a heated serving dish on the croûtes of bread and pour the sauce over the top. Arrange the mushrooms on either side of the dish and serve sprinkled with chopped parsley.

Langue de boeuf chasseur
Ox tongue with chasseur sauce

1 ox tongue, salted
1 carrot
1 onion
1 stick celery
1 bay leaf
6 peppercorns
¾ pint (approx. 2 cups) sauce chasseur (see recipe page 16)
pommes mousseline (see recipe page 88)
serves 6

Soak the tongue in cold water to cover for 8 hours or overnight. Place in a large saucepan with water to well cover, together with the whole cleaned vegetables, the bay leaf and the peppercorns. Bring to the boil slowly, cover and simmer for 4 hours. Allow to cool for 1 hour in the saucepan, then remove from the pan, skin, remove any bones and allow to cool.
Slice the tongue and place in a saucepan with the sauce chasseur. Reheat very gently. Arrange the pommes mousseline on a heated serving dish, top with the slices of ox tongue and pour the remaining sauce over the top.

Ragoût de queue de boeuf
Oxtail stew

1 × 3 lb. oxtail
2 onions
4 carrots
2 sticks celery
1 oz. (2T) butter
1 tablespoon (1¼T) oil
2 rashers streaky bacon, diced
1 oz. (¼ cup) plain (all purpose) flour
2 pints (5 cups) fond brun (beef bone stock, see recipe page 30)
bouquet garni
salt and pepper
1 turnip
10 shallots or small onions
1 small cabbage
chopped parsley for garnish

serves 4

Ask the butcher to chop through the oxtail at the joints. Put them in a bowl with cold water to cover and soak them overnight. Next day, place them in a saucepan, cover with fresh water and bring slowly to the boil, skimming the top as necessary. Simmer for 10–15 minutes. Drain well.
Slice the onions, 2 of the carrots and the celery. Heat the oil and butter in a large heavy saucepan, add the oxtail and brown very well all over. Remove from the pan. Place the prepared vegetables and the bacon in the saucepan and fry them until they begin to brown. Pour off the excess fat and add the flour, then cook, stirring, until the flour is a light brown. Add the stock, bouquet garni and salt and pepper to taste. Bring to the boil, stirring constantly.
Return the oxtail to the pan, cover and simmer very gently for 3–4 hours or until very tender.
Meanwhile, cut the remaining carrots and the turnip into ½ inch dice. Peel the shallots and leave whole. Place in a small saucepan of boiling, salted water and cook until tender. Drain well. Remove the outer leaves from the cabbage and cut the heart into quarters. Cook the cabbage in boiling, salted water until tender. Drain well. Remove the cooked oxtail from the gravy and place on a heated serving plate, piled high. Strain the gravy into a clean saucepan, bring to the boil, skin and boil rapidly until thickening slightly. Pour the gravy over the oxtail and garnish with the prepared vegetables around the edge and the parsley sprinkled over the top.

Veal stew (above)   Coq au vin (right)

Poultry and game

Poultry and game have always been popular in France, especially for peasant cookery, as poultry are kept on the local farms and wild game used to abound in the countryside. Some of the greatest French classic dishes will be found in this chapter; they include such favourites as chicken Marengo and coq-au-vin. Other less known recipes are included, such as partridge with cabbage, which has its origin in peasant cookery and was cooked when the man of the house brought home two partridges, one young and tender, the other old and tough. This recipe is a good solution to the cook's problem of how to cook them both to perfection.

All poultry, chicken, turkey, goose and duck are now all easily available, and can be bought ready-drawn and trussed for the oven, all the year round. Game is usually only available in season. It is possible to buy this, too, ready prepared. You may have to pluck and draw game yourself if you are presented with a newly killed bird, however, First, hang the birds for a week or ten days and then prepare them for the oven. Hares should also be hung for about this time before skinning. Collect the blood, if possible, for thickening the gravy.

Poultry and game, but game in particular, are rich and filling. Try to serve them with vegetables and accompaniments which will contrast both the texture and the flavour. Salads are crisp and light and make an ideal accompaniment. Fruit jellies and sauces, which are slightly tart, are a good foil for the rich meat.

Poulet à la vallée d'auge

Chicken with apples and cider

1 × 3–3½ lb. chicken
4 oz. (8T) butter
6 firm apples
salt and pepper
¾ oz. (3 tablespoons) plain (all purpose) flour
¾ pint (scant 2 cups) draught cider (hard)
bouquet garni
¼ pint (⅝ cup) double (heavy) cream
chopped parsley for garnish

serves 4

The Vallée d'Auge is a region in Normandy to the North of France.

Cut the chicken into 4 portions. Melt 2 oz. (4T) of the butter in a flameproof casserole, add the chicken and brown the portions all over. Remove and drain.
Peel, core and slice 2 of the apples, sprinkle with salt and pepper and fry in melted butter until beginning to brown. Sprinkle in the flour and cook gently, stirring occasionally until the flour is a light brown. Add ½ pint (1¼ cups) of the (hard) cider and bring to the boil, stirring constantly. Replace the chicken pieces and add the bouquet garni. Cover with greaseproof paper and a tightly fitting lid. Cook in a moderately hot oven (375°F. Mark 5) for 1 hour.
Meanwhile, peel, core and cut into quarters the remaining 4 apples. Melt 1 oz. (2T) butter in a frying pan and fry the apple until browned lightly. Place in an ovenproof dish with 3 tablespoons (¼ cup) water. Cover and place in the oven under the casserole, until needed.
When the chicken is cooked, remove it from the casserole and place it on a heated serving dish, to keep hot. Bring the sauce to the boil, add the remaining ¼ pint (⅝cup) of the (hard) cider, return to the boil and boil rapidly for 10 minutes. Strain and return to the rinsed saucepan. Add the apples and the cream. Stir in the remaining 1 oz. (2T) butter in small pieces. Reheat very gently without boiling Adjust seasoning. Pour over the chicken.
Serve garnished with chopped parsley.

Poulet à la marengo

Chicken Marengo

1 × 3–3½ chicken
3 tablespoons (¼ cup) oil
½ pint (1¼ cups) sauce espagnole (see recipe page 16)
8 oz. tomatoes, skinned, deseeded and chopped
1 clove garlic, crushed
3 tablespoons (¼ cup) sherry
12 button mushrooms
4 croûtes of fried bread
chopped parsley for garnish

This famous French classic is thus named because it was first eaten by Napoleon after the battle of Marengo in 1800.

Cut the chicken into 4 portions. Heat the oil in a large frying pan and fry the chicken on both sides until golden. Drain, keep warm. Prepare the sauce espagnole, then add the tomatoes and garlic. Bring to the boil and simmer, stirring occasionally, for 10 minutes. Add the sherry and cook for a further 5 minutes. Add the mushrooms and fry the chicken on both sides until golden. Drain, keep warm. Place the croûtes of bread on a heated serving dish, placing a chicken quarter on each.
Pour the sauce over and serve sprinkled with chopped parsley.

Poulet veronique

Chicken with grapes

2 oz. (4T) butter
4 chicken breasts
1 onion, chopped
1 pint (2½ cups) fond blanc de volaille (chicken stock, see recipe page 30)
1 oz. (¼ cup) plain (all purpose) flour
½ pint (1¼ cups) white wine
salt and pepper
2 oz. (1 cup) white grapes, peeled, halved and pipped
¼ pint (⅝ cup) soured cream
extra white grapes for garnish

serves 4

Melt 1 oz. (2T) of the butter in a large saucepan and fry the chicken breasts until lightly browned. Add the onion and the chicken stock. Bring to the boil and simmer, covered, for 30 minutes. Drain and reserve the stock.
Melt the remaining 1 oz. (2T) butter in a clean saucepan, stir in the flour off the heat and blend in ¼ pint (⅝ cup) of the reserved stock. Bring to the boil, stirring continuously and cook for 1 minute. Stir in the wine, seasonings, grapes and soured cream.
Reheat carefully, without boiling, stirring constantly.
Arrange the chicken breasts on a serving dish and coat evenly with the sauce. Serve garnished with the extra grapes.

Poulet paysan
Chicken peasant-style

1 × **3–4 lb. boiling fowl**
3 carrots
3 onions
bouquet garni
6 black peppercorns
salt
3 oz. (6T) butter
2 oz. mushrooms, sliced
2 leeks
clove garlic, crushed
2 rashers streaky bacon, diced
1 oz. (¼ cup) plain (all purpose) flour
¼ pint (⅝ cup) red wine
1 tomato, skinned, deseeded and chopped
1 turnip

serves 4–6

Place the chicken in a large saucepan and cover with water. Add 1 carrot, 1 onion, bouquet garni, peppercorns and 1 teaspoon salt. Cover the pan, bring to the boil and simmer for 1 hour. Drain, reserving the cooking liquor (liquid).
Melt 2 oz. (4T) of the butter in a large saucepan. Fry the chicken gently all over until golden. Remove and drain. Reserve the stock. Slice 1 carrot and 1 onion into thin slices and add to the saucepan with the mushrooms, leeks, garlic and bacon. Fry for 5–7 minutes. Add the flour and cook, stirring, 2–3 minutes. Add the wine, tomato, and 1 pint (2½ cups) of the chicken stock. Bring to the boil, stirring, add the chicken, cover and simmer slowly or cook in a moderate oven (350°F. Mark 4) for 1 hour or until the chicken is tender.
Slice the remaining carrot and onion into very thin rounds and slice the turnip thinly. Melt the remaining 1 oz. (2T) butter in a saucepan, add the prepared vegetables and ½ pint (1¼ cups) chicken stock. Cover and simmer very gently until the vegetables are tender, about 20 minutes. Drain.
Carve the chicken in large pieces: wings, drumsticks, breast. Place on a serving dish and keep warm. Strain the gravy into a saucepan, bring to the boil and boil rapidly until it begins to thicken. Pour the gravy over the chicken and place the vegetables in rows down each side of the chicken.
Serve very hot.

Poulet à la doria
Chicken with cucumber

Roast the chicken as above using half stock and half white wine in the roasting pan. Peel and chop 1 cucumber. Peel and trim 6 spring onions. Blanche them in boiling water, then cook in 1 oz. (2T) butter over a very low heat until soft and very tender. Stir in 1 tablespoon chopped mint.
Carve the chicken and serve garnished with the cucumber and spring onions on a heated serving plate. If liked, thicken the gravy with a little arrowroot and pour over the chicken. Otherwise serve it separately in a gravy boat.

Coq-au-vin
Chicken in red wine

1 × **3–3½ lb.**
3 oz. (6T) butter
8 small onions or shallots
4 rashers streaky bacon
3 tablespoons (¼ cup) brandy
½ pint (1¼ cups) red wine
½ pint (1¼ cups) chicken stock (see recipe page 30)
salt and freshly ground black pepper
bouquet garni
2 cloves garlic, crushed
4 oz. button mushrooms
1 oz. (¼ cup) plain (all purpose) flour
chopped parsley and fried croûtes of bread for garnish

serves 4

Translated literally, coq means cockerel. It is, however, permissable to use any chicken – not just a young cock!

Cut the chicken into 4 portions. Melt 2 oz. (4T) of the butter in a large saucepan and fry the chicken until golden, then remove and drain. Peel the onions, remove the rind and dice the bacon. Fry the onions and bacon in butter until golden, stirring occasionally. Return the chicken to the pan, pour in the brandy and ignite. When the flames have died down add the wine, stock, salt, freshly ground pepper, bouquet garni, garlic and mushrooms. Bring to the boil, cover, and simmer gently for 35–45 minutes or until the chicken is tender. Remove, and discard the bouquet garni.
Mix the remaining butter with the flour to a smooth paste (beurre manié). Remove the chicken from saucepan and place the portions on a heated serving plate, keeping hot. Bring the cooking liquor (liquid) to the boil and add the beurre manié in small pieces, stirring constantly. Add enough beurre manié to form a slightly thickened consistency. Allow the gravy to boil for 2–3 minutes.
Pour the gravy over the chicken, sprinkle with chopped parsley and arrange the croûtes around the edge of the plate. Serve very hot.

Poulet bonne femme
Chicken with white wine and mushrooms

1 × 3–3½ lb. chicken
2 oz. (4T) butter
12 small onions or shallots
4 oz. bacon, diced
½ oz. (2 tablespoons) plain (all purpose) flour
4 oz. button mushrooms
¼ pint (⅝ cup) white wine
¼ pint (⅝ cup) chicken stock (see recipe page 30
bouquet garni
salt and freshly ground black pepper
chopped parsley and croûtes of fried bread for garnish, optional
serves 4

Cut into 4 portions. Melt the butter in a large saucepan and fry the chicken pieces until brown all over. Remove and drain. Add the onions and bacon and fry until softened. Add the flour and cook, stirring, for 2–3 minutes. Add the mushrooms, wine, stock, bouquet garni, salt and pepper.
Bring to the boil and simmer for 35–45 minutes or until the chicken is tender.
Remove and discard the bouquet garni. Serve the chicken in a heated dish, pouring over the sauce and garnishing with chopped parsley and croûtes, if desired.

Poulet rôti au beurre
Chicken roasted in butter

1 × 3–3½ lb. chicken
salt and pepper
few sprigs rosemary or tarragon
2 oz. (4T) butter
2 rashers streaky bacon
½ pint (1¼ cups) chicken stock (made from giblets)

serves 4

Wipe the chicken and season inside with salt and pepper. Put sprigs of rosemary and tarragon into the bird with ½ oz. (1T) of the butter. Truss the chicken and rub the outside with the remaining butter. Place the chicken in a roasting pan, remove the rind from the bacon and place it across the breast. Pour the stock into the base of the pan. Roast in a moderate oven (350°F. Mark 4) for 20 minutes per lb. Turn the chicken over twice during the cooking time so that it will be evenly browned. Baste occasionally.
Strain the juices in the cooking pan into a small saucepan, bring to the boil and boil rapidly for 3–4 minutes. Skim. Serve in a gravy boat. Serve the chicken on a heated serving plate, ready for carving.

Vol-au-vent au volaille

Chicken vol-au-vent

8 oz. pâte feuilletée (see recipe page 119)
1 egg, beaten
8 oz. (2 cups) cold cooked chicken
½ pint (1¼ cups) sauce béchamel
1 egg yolk
juice of half a lemon
4 oz. button mushrooms
1 oz. butter
¼ teaspoon ground nutmeg
salt and pepper to taste

Roll out the pastry on a lightly floured board to ½ inch thickness. Use a saucepan lid of 6–7 inch diameter and place a sharp knife into the pastry. Cut round the lid with the knife sloping slightly outwards. Turn the round over and place on a damp baking tray. Make a circle in the middle of the round, using smaller saucepan lid or a saucer as a guide, but cut only half way through the pastry. Mark a criss-cross pattern on the centre circle with a knife. Allow the pastry to rest in a cool place for 20 minutes before baking. Brush the top with beaten egg and then bake in a very hot oven (475°F. Mark 8) for 10 minutes. Reduce the oven temperature to moderately hot (375°F. Mark 5) for a further 10–15 minutes or until cooked. Meanwhile cut the chicken into bite sized pieces. Prepare the sauce béchamel, add the egg yolk and reheat without boiling. Stir in the chicken and lemon juice. Melt the butter in a small saucepan, add the mushrooms and fry gently for 3–5 minutes. Add the mushrooms to the sauce, reheat, and season with nutmeg, salt and pepper. Remove the centre circle from the vol-au-vent, being careful not to break it. Scoop out the pastry in the centre and spoon in the sauce. Replace the lid.
Serve immediately, on a heated serving dish.

serves 4

note: do not reheat the completed dish or the pastry may become soggy.

Vol-au-vents au volaille et poires

Chicken and pear vol-au-vents

Cut the pâte feuilleté into 4 rounds each 2–2½ inches diameter. Mark and glaze as above, bake in a very hot oven (425°F. Mark 7) for 20–25 minutes. Prepare the chicken filling as above. Peel, core and chop 1 lb. pears and add them to the sauce in place of the mushrooms (add them raw; do not fry them in butter first). Reheat, serve as above.

Canard à la rouennaise

Duck Rouen-style

1 × 4 lb. duck
2 rashers streaky bacon
salt and pepper
1 shallot, chopped
1½ oz. (3T) butter
4 oz. liver pâté
¼ pint (⅝ cup) sauce espagnole (see recipe page 16)
¼ pint (⅝ cup) red wine
fried croûtons for garnish

Rouen is a large town of the North of France in the Normandy area. It is greatly famed for its ducks and, naturally, has its own special recipe for cooking them. Rouen ducks are much more gamey than those we usually buy and the meat is darker in colour. If you buy a good fresh duck, you will still make a delicious dish.

Remove the legs from the duck. Place the duck in a roasting pan with the legs separate. Place the rashers of bacon over the duck and sprinkle with salt and pepper. Roast in a very hot oven (450°F. Mark 7) for about 45 minutes to 1 hour or until the duck is almost cooked but still slightly underdone.
Melt ½ oz. (1T) of the butter in a frying pan and cook the duck liver with the shallot until softened and tender. Mix together thoroughly the shallot, the liver, the remaining butter and the pâté.
Mix the sauce espagnole with red wine, heat until boiling and simmer 2–3 minutes.
Carve the duck. Place the pâté mixture down the centre of a heated serving plate, arranging the carved duck (and the legs) on each side.

serves 4

Pour the sauce over the duck and serve sprinkled with croûtons.

Canard à l'orange — Duck with orange

1 × 4 lb. duck
2 oz. (4T) butter
½ pint (1¼ cups) water
¼ pint (⅝ cup) white wine
salt and pepper
1 bay leaf
3 oranges
1 tablespoon (1¼T) arrowroot

serves 4

Wipe the duck and truss it. Place it on a rack in a roasting pan, prick the skin in 6 or 8 places and rub with butter. Place the water and wine in the base of the pan with a sprinkling of salt and pepper, the bay leaf and the zest of 1 orange (use a potato peeler to peel the zest off in strips). Roast the duck in a moderately hot oven (375°F. Mark 5) for 30 minutes, then reduce the temperature to moderately slow (325°F. Mark 3) for 1¼–1½ hours (allowing 25–30 minutes cooking time for each lb.).

Place the duck on a serving plate and keep hot. Strain the cooking liquor (liquid) into a saucepan and make up to ¾ pint (approx. 2 cups) with water. Add the juice of 2 oranges and the rind of 1 orange cut into matchstick strips. Mix a little of the water with the arrowroot and add to sauce. Bring to the boil, stirring constantly and simmer 3–4 minutes.

Garnish the duck with slices of orange. Pour a little of the sauce over the duck. Serve hot with the remaining sauce in a sauce boat.

note: the giblets can be used to make stock which can then be used instead of water.

If the orange rind is tough, blanche the matchstick strips in boiling water before adding them to the sauce.

Chicken with apples and cider
(below)

Chicken and pear vol-au-vent
(above right)

Duck with orange (below right)

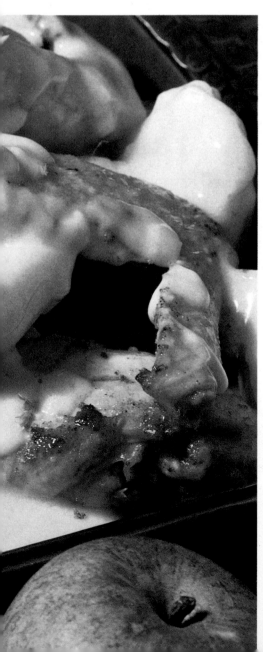

Dinde rôti   Roast turkey

1 × 8 lb. turkey
4 oz. (8T) butter
parsley
salt and freshly ground black pepper
½ tablespoon (1T) melted butter
1 tablespoon plain (all purpose) flour

Truss the turkey and rub well with 3 oz. (6T) of the butter. Put the remaining butter, with some sprigs of parsley, into the bird. Season the turkey with salt and freshly ground black pepper. Place the turkey in a roasting pan with the giblets (not the liver) and ½ inch depth of water. Roast, covered with greased greaseproof paper or aluminium foil, in a moderately hot oven (375°F. Mark 5) for 2 hours 40 minutes (allowing 20 minutes cooking time for each lb.). It may be necessary to add more water to the pan during the cooking. Remove the paper or foil after 2 hours.
Place the cooked turkey on a serving plate and keep hot. Discard the giblets. Place the melted butter in a frying pan and cook the liver gently until tender. Skim off 1 tablespoon (2T) butter from the turkey and mix it with the flour to make a paste. Return the paste to the gravy, bring to the boil, stirring constantly and simmer 3–4 minutes. Add the liver, sliced thinly.

serves 10   Serve hot with the gravy in a gravy boat.

Oie rôtie à la périgord   Roast goose Périgord-style

1 × 8 lb. goose
salt and pepper
3 lb. potatoes, peeled and quartered
5 hard-boiled eggs
watercress for garnish

Goose is considered a great delicacy in some parts of France. In Strasbourg, as in the Périgord region, geese are fattened for their liver to make pâté de foie gras. The livers can weigh from 1½ to 2½ lb. each. The actual geese, however, tend to be small.

Truss the goose and sprinkle it with salt and pepper. Place it on a rack in a large roasting pan. Cover with greased greaseproof paper or aluminium foil and roast in a moderately slow oven (325°F. Mark 3) for 3–3½ hours (allowing 25 minutes cooking time for each lb.) Remove the paper for the last 30 minutes.
Cook the potatoes in boiling salted water for 5 minutes, drain. When the goose has been cooking for about 1½–2 hours, pour off most of the fat in the roasting pan and add the potatoes.
Cut the eggs into quarters and add them to the roasting pan 10 minutes before cooking time is complete.
Drain the cooked potatoes and eggs. Serve the goose on a heated
serves 10   serving plate surrounded with eggs and potatoes.

Lapin sauté chasseur   Fried rabbit hunter-style

1 young rabbit
salt and pepper
flour
1 oz. (2T) butter
2 tablespoons (2½T) oil
2 shallots, chopped
½ tablespoon (¾T) plain (all purpose) flour
¼ pint (⅝ cup) red wine
¼ pint (⅝ cup) fond blanc (white stock, see recipe page 30)
1 tomato, skinned, deseeded and chopped
1 clove garlic, crushed
bouquet garni
4 oz. button mushrooms, sliced
croûtons of fried bread
chopped parsley for garnish
serves 4

Cut the rabbit into joints, wash it in cold salted water, then rinse and dry it. Mix the salt and pepper with flour and coat the rabbit pieces. Heat the butter and oil in a large saucepan, add the rabbit and fry it until it is golden all over. Remove the rabbit and drain. Add the shallots, cook, stirring, until softened. Stir in ½ tablespoon (¾T) flour and cook 2–3 minutes. Add the wine, stock, tomato, garlic, bouquet garni and salt and pepper.
Return the rabbit to the pan, cover and simmer gently for 30 minutes. Add the mushrooms and cook for another 10 minutes or until rabbit is cooked. Remove the bouquet garni.
Serve sprinkled with croûtons and chopped parsley.

84

Pigeons en cocotte normande
Casseroled pigeons with apples and cider

4 small pigeons
1½ oz. (3T) butter
1 tablespoon (1¼T) oil
1 onion, sliced
4 apples
1 oz. (¼ cup) plain (all purpose) flour
¾ pint (scant 2 cups) water
½ pint (1¼ cups) cider (hard)
salt and pepper
bouquet garni
4 rashers streaky bacon, grilled
chopped parsley for garnish

Pigeons which are young, plump, have supple bones and a rosy red skin are suitable for roasting. Rub each pigeon with butter, season well and roast in a hot oven for 25–35 minutes. Too frequently, however, pigeons are not suitable for roasting. Try cooking them in the following way and they will be both tender and delicious.

Wipe the pigeons. Heat 1 oz. (2T) of the butter and the oil in a large saucepan, add the pigeons and fry until they are browned all over. Remove and drain. Fry the onion, peel and core and slice one apple and add it to the saucepan. Fry the onion and apple until golden, remove and drain. Add the flour to the pan and cook over a low heat, stirring, until cooked and beginning to brown. Add the water and cider, bring to the boil, and simmer 2–3 minutes.
Place the pigeons in an ovenproof casserole, adding the onion, apple, sauce, salt and pepper and bouquet garni. Cover and cook in a moderate oven (350°F. Mark 4) for 1½ hours.
Peel, core and slice the remaining apples into rings, heat the remaining ½ oz. (1T) butter in a frying pan and cook the apple rings until golden.
Remove the cooked pigeons from the casserole. Strain the sauce into a saucepan, bring to the boil and boil rapidly until reduced in quantity and thickening.
Arrange the pigeons on a heated serving dish, pour over the sauce and garnish with the apple rings, crisp bacon and chopped parsley.

Perdrix au chou
Partridge with cabbage

2 large partridges
1 small, firm, green cabbage
6 oz. fat bacon (in one piece)
4 carrots, sliced
2 onions, sliced
4 oz. pork sausage (charcuterie)
salt and pepper
6 juniper berries
2 cloves garlic, crushed
¼ teaspoon ground nutmeg
fond brun (white stock, see recipe page 30)
1 tablespoon (1¼T) arrowroot

This is a classic 'cuisine bourgeoise' recipe. It is an ideal way of cooking two partridges if one is young and tender and the other old.

Wipe the partridges. Cut the cabbage in quarters and blanche in boiling salted water for 3–4 minutes then slice each quarter in thin slices. Slice the bacon thickly, fry a little in a large saucepan, add the partridges and brown all over.
Put a layer of cabbage in the base of a large ovenproof dish, top with the remaining bacon slices, carrots, onions, sausages and the partridges. Season with salt and pepper, add the juniper berries, garlic, nutmeg and enough stock to almost cover the vegetables. Cover with the remaining cabbage.
Cover the dish with greased greaseproof paper and then a tight lid. Cook in a moderately slow oven (325°F. Mark 3) for about 2 hours. The cabbage must be cooked for the whole time but the other ingredients may be cooked sooner. If one partridge is young, remove it from the dish after about 40 minutes; remove the sausages after 30 minutes; remove the bacon after 45 minutes. Return all the ingredients to the dish about 15 minutes before cooking time is completed to allow them to heat through.
Drain all the cooked ingredients, including the cabbage, and carve the partridges. Keep them hot.
Thicken the remaining stock with arrowroot. Mix the arrowroot with a little of the stock, put the remainder in a saucepan, add the arrowroot, bring to the boil and simmer for 2–3 minutes.
Arrange the cabbage and other vegetables on a heated serving plate, putting the carved partridges on top. Pour a little sauce over the cabbage. Serve the remainder separately in a sauce boat.

serves 4

Civet de lièvre landais Jugged hare Landes-style

1 hare
2 oz. (¼ cup) pork fat
10 shallots, peeled
2 cloves garlic, crushed
4 oz. Bayonne ham, diced
¼ pint (⅝ cup) red wine
½ pint (1¼ cups) water
**4 tomatoes, skinned, deseeded
and chopped**
1 oz. dried cèpes
**salt and freshly ground
black pepper**
**croûtes of fried bread
for serving**

This is a traditional recipe from the Landes department in the South West of France. Bayonne ham should be used, but gammon makes a good substitute. The recipe also includes cèpes which are a type of edible fungus. They are available dried in some shops but, if unavailable, use 2 oz. mushrooms instead.

Cut the hare into serving portions and wash well in cold water. Heat the pork fat in a large saucepan and fry the hare until browned all over. Remove the hare, drain and place it in an ovenproof casserole. Brown the shallots in pork fat and add them to the casserole. Fry the garlic and ham until golden, drain and place in the casserole. Add the remaining ingredients—the wine, water, tomatoes, cèpes and salt and pepper to the casserole.
Cover the casserole tightly and cook in a moderately slow oven (325°F. Mark 3) for 1½–2 hours or until the hare is very tender. Place the hare on a heated serving dish. Strain the sauce into a saucepan, bring to the boil and boil rapidly until it has thickened slightly. Pour the sauce over the hare and serve garnished with croûtes of fried bread around the edge.

note: if you are lucky enough to have some of the hare's blood, add some of it to the sauce to thicken it, just before serving.

serves 6

Jugged hare (above)   *Stuffed tomatoes and ratatouille (right)*

Vegetables

The French have great respect for their vegetables. Meat, being very expensive, is often replaced by vegetables which can provide almost as much nutritious value. In other cases, carefully prepared vegetables make a very attractive garnish to a meat dish, even giving the dish its name. Fresh spring vegetables, cut into matchstick strips and cooked, give the dish they garnish the name 'julienne'. The same vegetables diced give the name 'brunoise'. A chateaubriand steak has its name because it is always served with a garnish of château potatoes. Always buy first quality vegetables. If fresh are unavailable, use frozen vegetables as these are usually in peak condition. Vegetables, raw or cooked, generally freeze very well, so if you cook too much of one dish, try freezing the remainder for a later date (ratatouille freezes especially well, so make a double or treble quantity).

Except when used as a garnish, vegetables are usually served as a separate course to the meat, either before or after the main course. All the vegetables, however, can also be served with the meat, as we are familiar with this method. Some of these versatile recipes can also be served as hors d'oeuvres.

Pommes château
Château potatoes

1–1½ lbs. potatoes
2 oz. (4T) clarified butter
salt
parsley

serves 4

Peel the potatoes and shape them into small pieces the size and shape of large olives. Cook them in boiling water for 1 minute, drain and dry well.
Melt the butter in a large frying pan, add the potatoes and cook gently, carefully shaking the pan occasionally, until the potatoes are cooked and golden. Drain.
Serve either in a heated dish or as a garnish, sprinkled with salt and finely chopped parsley.

Pommes parisienne
Parisienne potatoes

The potatoes used in the above recipe should be cut into balls about ¼–½ inch in diameter using a ball-cutter. Pommes parisienne are then cooked in exactly the same way as pommes château.

Pommes mousseline
Potato purée

2 lb. potatoes
2 oz. (4T) butter
approximately ¼ pint (⅝ cup) hot milk
salt and pepper

serves 4–6

Wash the potatoes, place in a saucepan of water with enough cold water to cover. Bring to the boil and simmer for about 20 minutes or until tender. Drain thoroughly. Remove the skins.
Add the butter to the potatoes in small pieces and beat well. Gradually add the milk until the potatoes are soft, smooth and creamy. Season with salt and pepper to taste. Reheat gently over a low heat.
Serve as required.

Pommes mousseline provençale

Make pommes mousseline as above. The meat juices from a joint cooked 'à la Provençale' (i.e. with garlic and herbs) are then poured around the edge of the potato on the serving plate.
In France, this dish is sometimes eaten as a separate course before the meat.

Pommes de terre à la savoyarde
Potatoes with cheese

1 lb. potatoes
½ pint (1¼ cups) fond blanc (white stock, see recipe page 30)
1 egg, beaten
salt and pepper
¼ teaspoon grated nutmeg
2 oz. (½ cup) grated gruyère cheese
1 clove garlic
1 oz. (2T) butter
serves 4

Peel and slice the potatoes finely. Put them in a bowl and add the stock with the egg beaten into it. Season with salt, pepper and nutmeg. Add the grated cheese and mix thoroughly.
Grease an ovenproof dish and rub it with a cut clove of garlic. Add the potato mixture and dot with small pieces of butter. Cook in a moderately slow oven (325°F. Mark 3) for 35–40 minutes or until the potato is cooked and the top beginning to brown. Serve in the dish in which it is cooked.

Pommes de terre à la dauphinoise
Potatoes with milk and cheese

Prepare the potatoes as above but substitute milk for the white stock.

Pommes de terre à la lyonnaise
Fried potatoes with onions

1½ lb. potatoes
2 onions
4 oz. (8T) butter
salt
chopped parsley for garnish

serves 4–6

Wash the potatoes and boil them in their skins until tender. Skin them and cut into ¼ inch slices. Peel and slice the onions thinly. Melt 2 oz. (4T) of the butter in a large frying pan and fry the potato slices until golden brown all over, about 15–20 minutes. In a separate frying pan, melt the remaining 2 oz. (4T) butter and fry the onion rings, stirring, until golden, about 10 minutes.
Drain the potatoes and onion thoroughly, sprinkle with salt and mix together gently. Serve in a heated dish, sprinkled with chopped parsley.

Pommes duchesse
Duchess potatoes

1½ lb. potatoes
2 egg yolks
3 tablespoons (¼ cup) milk or single (light) cream
1 oz. (2T) butter
salt and pepper
¼ teaspoon ground nutmeg
beaten egg for glazing

serves 4–6

Wash the potatoes and boil them in their skins until tender. Skin, then press them through a sieve. Return them to a clean saucepan, add the egg yolks, cream, butter, salt, pepper, and nutmeg.
Heat the saucepan very gently and beat the potatoes thoroughly until light and fluffy.
Place the beaten potatoes in a forcing bag with a large star piping tube. Pipe rosettes of potato on to a greased baking tray and brush them lightly with beaten egg.
Bake in a hot oven (425°F. Mark 7) until golden. (The time will vary according to the size of the rosettes.) Serve as required.

Pommes croquettes
Croquette potatoes

½ quantity duchess potatoes (see above)
flour
beaten egg
breadcrumbs (soft or dried – both are suitable)
oil for deep frying

serves 4

Divide the prepared potato into 8 pieces. Shape each piece on a lightly floured board into a cork shape, slightly narrower at one end. Roll the croquettes in flour.
Dip each croquette in beaten egg, then in breadcrumbs. Repeat the process. Deep fry in hot oil (375°F. or until a ¼ inch dice of bread will brown in less than a minute) until crisp and golden.
Drain thoroughly on absorbent kitchen paper. Serve hot.

note: croquettes can be made in practically any shape. Cork-shaped croquettes are traditional.

Carottes vichy
Carrots Vichy

1 lb. carrots
2 oz. (4T) butter
1 teaspoon sugar
pinch of salt
chopped parsley for garnish

serves 4

Peel the carrots and slice thinly. Melt 1 oz. of the butter in a heavy saucepan, add the sugar, salt, carrots and ¾ pint (scant 2 cups) water. Bring to the boil and simmer, uncovered, until the carrots are cooked and the liquid has evaporated. Add the remaining butter and toss the carrots lightly.
Serve in a heated dish sprinkled with chopped parsley.

Choufleur polonaise
Cauliflower polonaise

1 cauliflower
salt
2 oz. (4T) butter
3 tablespoons (¼ cup) dry white breadcrumbs
1 hard boiled egg
chopped parsley for garnish

serves 4

Break the cauliflower into florets and soak in cold salted water for 20 minutes. Cook the cauliflower in a large saucepan of boiling salted water for 15 minutes or until tender. Drain thoroughly.
Place the cauliflower florets in a heated serving dish. Melt the butter in a frying pan and fry the breadcrumbs until golden, then sprinkle them over the cauliflower.
Chop the egg yolk and egg white separately. Sprinkle the yolk on to the cauliflower and place the white at each end.
Serve hot, sprinkled with chopped parsley.

Courgettes aux amandes

Courgettes (zucchini) with almonds

1 lb. courgettes (zucchini)
flour
salt and pepper
3 oz. (6T) butter
2 oz. ($\frac{1}{3}$ cup) almonds, split
$\frac{1}{4}$ pint ($\frac{5}{8}$ cup) single (light) cream

serves 4

Wash the courgettes (zucchini) and cut into $\frac{1}{2}$ inch slices. Toss the slices in flour seasoned with salt and pepper. Melt the butter in a frying pan, add the courgettes and fry until golden on both sides. Drain.
Arrange the courgettes in a heated serving dish. Fry the almonds in butter until beginning to brown. Drain and sprinkle over the courgettes.
Heat the cream gently, season with salt and pepper and pour over the courgettes. Serve as soon as possible.

Onions used in cooking (above)   *Potatoes with cheese (right)*

Cassoulet Beanstew

8 oz. haricot beans
4 oz. pickled pork
2 cloves garlic, crushed
4 oz. lamb
2 tablespoons olive oil
1 onion, sliced
bouquet garni
salt and pepper
2 oz. sausage (pork or garlic are both suitable)
2 large tomatoes, skinned, deseeded and chopped
chopped parsley for garnish

serves 4

This dish comes from the Languedoc region of France, although most of the regions have now adapted it for their own. The name cassoulet comes from a small town in Languedoc called Cassol d'Issel where the traditional clay cooking pot for this dish originated.

Soak the beans overnight in water to cover, drain the following day. Place the pork, garlic and lamb in a small saucepan with cold water to cover, bring to the boil and simmer for 5–7 minutes. Drain the meat slice.
Heat the oil in a flameproof casserole, fry the pork and lamb with the onion until golden. Add the beans, bouquet garni, salt and pepper and enough boiling water to almost cover the beans. Cover the casserole tightly and cook in a slow oven (300°F. Mark 2) for 2½–3 hours. Add the sliced sausage and tomatoes 1 hour before the cooking time is completed.
Remove the bouquet garni and serve sprinkled with chopped parsley.

Aubergines farcies provençale

Stuffed aubergines (eggplants) Provençale

2 aubergines (eggplants)
1 oz. (2T) butter
2 onions, chopped
2 tomatoes, skinned, deseeded
and chopped
½ teaspoon mixed chopped
dried herbs
salt and pepper
3 tablespoons (¼ cup)
grated cheese
4 anchovy fillets
olive oil

serves 4

Place the aubergines (eggplants) in a large saucepan of boiling water (to cover). Cook for 10 minutes. Cut in half lengthwise and scoop out the pulp, leaving about a ½ inch wall of skin. Chop the pulp into large pieces.

Melt the butter in a saucepan, add the onions and fry until softened. Add the tomatoes, herbs and salt and pepper. Cover and cook gently for 5 minutes. Add the chopped aubergine and reheat.

Pile the stuffing into the aubergine skin halves, sprinkle each with grated cheese and place an anchovy on top. Brush lightly with a little oil. Place the stuffed aubergines under a hot grill and cook until golden.

Arrange the aubergines on a heated serving dish and serve as soon as possible.

Stuffed aubergines (eggplants) Provençale   *Mediterranean vegetable stew*

Petits pois à la Française

Peas French-style

1 oz. (2T) butter
6 spring onions, sliced
6 lettuce leaves, shredded finely
¼ teaspoon salt
¼ teaspoon black pepper
1 sprig each parsley and mint
1 teaspoon sugar
1 lb. shelled peas
1 teaspoon plain (all
purpose) flour
2 teaspoons butter

serves 4

Melt the butter in a large saucepan, add the spring onions, lettuce, salt, pepper, parsley, mint, sugar and peas. Stir in ¼ pint (⅝ cup) water, bring to the boil, cover and simmer gently for about 20 minutes or until the peas are very tender.

Remove and discard the parsley and mint. Cream the flour and butter together thoroughly and add to the peas in small pieces. Stir gently with a wooden spoon and heat gently until any remaining liquid is thickened.

Serve piping hot.

Haricots verts au beurre
French beans in butter

1 lb. French beans
salt
1 oz. (2T) butter
freshly ground black pepper

serves 4

Tender young French beans are best served in the simplest way. They are easy to prepare, needing only to be topped and tailed.

Prepare the beans and cook them in a saucepan with 1 inch of boiling salted water, for 10–15 minutes. Drain well. Melt the butter in the saucepan, add the beans and toss until coated in butter. Serve in a heated dish and sprinkle generously with black pepper.

Ratatouille
Mediterranean vegetable stew

3 aubergines (eggplants)
3 courgettes (zucchini)
salt
3 red peppers
5 tomatoes
3 onions
¼ pint (⅝ cup) olive oil
2 cloves garlic, crushed
6 coriander seeds, crushed
1 teaspoon chopped dried parsley
½ teaspoon chopped dried basil
freshly ground black pepper
serves 6–8

Slice the aubergines (eggplants) and courgettes (zucchini) into ¼ inch rounds. Place in a colander, in layers, and sprinkle each layer with salt. Cover with a plate and leave for 45 minutes. Drain off excess moisture.
Remove the seeds and membranes from the peppers, cut into thin strips. Skin the tomatoes by immersing them in boiling water for 2 minutes, cool in cold water and peel off the skin. Cut into ½ inch slices. Peel and slice the onions thinly.
Heat the olive oil in a saucepan, add the onion and fry gently until softened but not browned. Add a layer of peppers, then aubergines, courgettes and finally tomatoes with the garlic and coriander seeds. Simmer very gently, covered, for 1–1¼ hours or until the vegetables are soft but not mushy.
Stir in the herbs (taste and add salt and pepper as necessary). Serve in a heated dish.

note: this dish keeps and can be successfully reheated. Mushrooms can also be included in a ratatouille. Add sliced mushrooms to the saucepan about 30 minutes before the cooking time is completed.

Oignons frites
Fried onion rings

1 lb. onions
2 egg whites
flour
salt and pepper
oil for deep frying
serves 4–6

Slice the onions thinly. Whisk the egg whites until frothy. Mix the flour with salt and pepper.
Dip each separate onion ring into egg white then into seasoned flour. Deep fry the rings (adding them individually to prevent them sticking together) in deep hot oil until golden and crisp. (The oil should be 375°F. or a ¼ inch dice of bread will brown in less than a minute.) Drain very thoroughly on absorbent kitchen paper.
Serve as required, piping hot.

Salade verte
Green salad

This salad is often called salade de saison (Seasonal Salad). Which ingredients are used depends on what is available. The following ingredients are all suitable: lettuce; endive; chicory; watercress; dandelion leaves; sorrel; celery; celeriac; cucumber; green pepper. The list is almost endless. Fresh herbs are also frequently included giving a really individual flavour to your salad. Try using one of the following: parsley; chives; lovage; chervil; mint.
Try to obtain vegetables as fresh as possible. Tear green leaves into bite sized pieces and cut other green vegetables into thin slices. Chop the herbs roughly.
Toss the vegetables in just enough sauce vinaigrette (see recipe page 21) to make each individual leaf glisten. Serve your salad as soon as it has been tossed or else it may become soggy.

Salade au chapon

Rub a slice of French bread all over with a cut clove of garlic and sprinkle each side with 1 teaspoon olive oil. Prepare a salad as above and toss the prepared bread into the salad with the dressing. The salad will have a slight but delicious flavour of garlic.

Salade niçoise   Salad from Nice

½ lettuce
½ head curly endive
1 onion, thinly sliced
2 tomatoes, skinned and sliced
¼ cucumber, sliced
1 green pepper, thinly sliced
12 black olives, pitted
4 anchovy fillets
1 × 7 oz. can tuna
1 tablespoon chopped fresh basil
1 clove garlic, crushed
sauce vinaigrette (see recipe
page 21)

This salad is served as an hors d'oeuvre in France but is more popular in other countries when served with the main course. Both methods are good. There are many different recipes but each one must include ingredients which are available along the French Mediterranean coast.

Wash, dry and tear the lettuce and endive into bite sized pieces. Prepare the vegetables and olives, cut the anchovy fillet in half lengthwise, drain the tuna and break into large pieces.
Place the vegetables, olives and fish in a salad bowl. Add the basil and garlic to the sauce vinaigrette and sprinkle over the salad. Toss all the ingredients together gently and serve immediately.

note: hard boiled eggs, cut into quarters, are frequently added to this salad to make it more substantial. Cooked French beans or tiny new potatoes make another delicious addition.

Mushroom soufflé (above)   Camembert cream (right)

Cheese and savouries

Cheese and savouries play a large part in a French dinner party menu. They are the 'bridge' between the main part of the meal and the sweet or dessert. Normally, cheese is served, but for a more elaborate meal a hot, freshly prepared savoury is delicious.

All the savouries can double as appetizers before a meal or simply with drinks at a cocktail party. They make a very welcome change from the well known canapés and bouchées.

The Cheeses of France

The French make delicious cheeses from both cow's and goat's milk. Some are mild, creamy cheeses while others can be strong and well-ripened.

Cream cheeses These are the very softest kind of cheese. The best known are Petit Suisse, Demi-sel and various herb cheeses (all made from cow's milk) which come from Normandy; Saint-Marcellin comes from Savoie and is made from a mixture of cow's and goat's milk, and Valancay from Touraine is also made from cow's milk.

Soft cheeses The most famous of this kind of cheese is Camembert, which is made from cow's milk, in the Normandy area. Another similar cheese, Livarot, is made in the same area; it is slightly larger in size and stronger in flavour than Camembert. Yet another is Pont-l'Evéque. Brie, again made from cow's milk, is made on the border of Champagne and Ile de France and both provinces claim it for their own. A goat's milk cheese which comes from the village of Sainte-Maure in Touraine and bears the same name as the village, also falls into this category. It does not keep well, though, and is not frequently seen outside France.

Semi-hard cheeses There are more French cheeses of this kind than of any other. The most well-known are St Paulin, Port Salut and Baby Bel from Normandy. Reblochon and Tome de Savoie (that is the one with the grape pip rind) are less well-known and come from the Haute Savoie province. Those cheeses already mentioned are all cow's milk cheeses, but there are also a few goat's milk semi-hard cheeses including Banon and Chèvre, the latter covering a whole range of anonymous goat's milk cheeses which are white, crumbly and mild.

Hard cheeses These are limited in number. One of the most famous is Munster cheese from Alsace; it has a strong flavour and creamy texture. Another is Cantal, a cow's milk cheese from Auvergne. This is similar to a mature cheddar cheese and will keep well.

Blue cheeses Roquefort is the undisputed king of French cheeses. It is crumbly with a green mould and made from ewe's milk, in the midi and sud-oest of France. The true Roquefort is always matured in the caves of Rouergue. Other blue cheeses are Bleu de Bresse and Bleu d'Auvergne, named after their places of origin.

There are of course many, many more French cheeses. Above are mentioned just some of the better known among them.

Always buy cheese with care. If it is wrapped in waxed paper or foil, make sure that the paper is not damaged or the cheese inside may be dry and spoiled. Cream cheeses are best when fresh or slightly mature. Blue cheeses are still at their best when very mature.

Make sure that the cheese you buy has been made in France and avoid imitations manufactured elsewhere. By means of refrigeration, cheese can now be kept fresh for a very long time, so French cheeses are obtainable throughout the world.

Store cheese carefully to keep it in good condition. Cream cheeses can be kept up to 4 days in the refrigerator. Soft cheeses will also keep well in a refrigerator as the cold arrests the ripening process. Outside a refrigerator they will only keep 2–3 days. All other cheeses should be stored in a cool larder or in the warmest part of the refrigerator. Wrap semi-hard cheeses in a damp cloth to keep them moist, and, after cutting, place them in a polythene bag or foil. Blue cheese should be placed in an airtight bag or box.

The French serve the cheese directly after the main course with the bread and butter left over from the meal. The dessert course follows the cheese. Cream cheese can be served straight from the refrigerator but other cheeses must be left at room temperature for at least an hour, or, in the case of Camembert or Brie, two hours. Serve the cheese whole, not cut up in any way, but unwrapped. Petit Suisse is unsalted and can be eaten with either salt or sugar. It is usual to serve a variety of cheeses for the diners to choose from. Make sure that they are not all the same texture but include at least one from each category, from cream to blue cheese.

Crème au camembert Camembert cream

3 × 1 oz. portions
Camembert cheese
½ oz. (1T) butter, melted
1 × ½ oz. portion Petit
Suisse cheese
3 tablespoons (¼ cup) double
(heavy) cream
1 teaspoon French mustard
1 teaspoon finely
chopped parsley
watercress for garnish
serves 4

Cut the rind off the Camembert, mix with the melted butter and beat well until smooth. Add the Petit Suisse and beat well. Lightly whip the cream and add to the cheese mixture with the French mustard and parsley. Mix well.
Pour the mixture into a small mould or serving dish. Chill. Serve unmoulded or in the dish, garnished with watercress.

Diablotine gruyère Devilled gruyère tarts

4 oz. pâte brisée (shortcrust
pastry, see recipe page 119)
1 oz. (1T) butter
½ oz. (2 tablespoons) cornflour
(cornstarch)
¼ pint (⅝ cup) milk
2 eggs
3 oz. (¾ cup) grated
gruyère cheese
salt and cayenne pepper
1 teaspoon anchovy paste

makes 1–1½ dozen

Make the pâte brisée and roll out thinly on to a lightly floured board. Line 12–18 small patty tins.
Melt the butter in a small saucepan, add the cornflour, then the milk, stirring constantly until the mixture is smooth. Bring to the boil, stirring, simmer 2–3 minutes. Remove the pan from the heat, beat in the egg yolks with 2 oz. (½ cup) of cheese, salt and cayenne pepper. Whisk the egg whites until stiff and fold into the cheese mixture.
Half fill the pastry cases with the egg mixture, put a spot of anchovy paste on top and cover with more egg mixture. Sprinkle with the remaining cheese. Bake the tarts in a moderately hot oven (375°F. Mark 5) for 15–20 minutes or until firm and golden brown. Serve piping hot.

Diables à cheval Stuffed prunes

8 prunes
8 almonds, toasted
4 rashers streaky bacon
8 small croûtes of fried bread
watercress to garnish

makes 8

Stone the prunes and place a toasted almond in each one. Remove the bacon rind and spread each rasher of bacon with the back of a knife until thin and almost doubled in length, then cut in half.
Wind a piece of bacon around each prune and secure with a wooden cocktail stick. Cook the stuffed prunes under a hot grill until the bacon is golden.
Serve each hot savoury on a croûte of fried bread, garnishing the plate with a sprig of watercress.

note: instead of almonds, try using a rolled up anchovy or a stuffed olive to stuff the prunes.

Aigrettes au fromage Cheese aigrettes

2 oz. (4T) butter
¼ pint (⅝ cup) water
2½ oz. (good ½ cup) plain (all
purpose) flour
2 eggs, beaten
2 oz. (½ cup) grated
Parmesan cheese
pinch of cayenne pepper
salt
deep oil for frying

Place the butter and water in a saucepan, then heat slowly until the butter is melted and the water is at boiling point. Remove from the heat. Add all the sifted flour and beat well with a wooden spoon until the mixture is smooth and falls away from the sides of the pan. Allow the paste to cool slightly, then add the beaten eggs gradually and mix well. Stir in the cheese and seasoning.
Heat the oil until 375°F. (a ¼ inch dice of bread will brown in less than a minute). Fry teaspoonfuls of the mixture until puffed up, golden and crisp, about 10 minutes. Drain well on absorbent kitchen paper. Sprinkle with salt.
Serve very hot piled on to a plate.

Éclairs savoureux   Savoury éclairs

Savoury éclairs in preparation

Filling savoury éclairs

Savoury éclairs

Savoury éclairs are an unusual and delicious hot or cold savoury. They can be made with the same paste used for cheese aigrettes, baked and not fried. Grease a baking tray and pipe 1–1½ inch lengths of the paste (use a ⅜ inch plain round pipe), brush the tops with beaten egg and bake in a hot oven (400°F. Mark 6) for about 25 minutes or until golden and crisp. Serve as soon as possible. Alternatively, omit the cheese from the recipe for cheese aigrettes and make and bake as above. Make a slit in the side of each éclair to let the steam out, then allow to cool. Fill each éclair with a savoury filling just before serving. The filling can be a pâté or even scrambled egg with ham—indeed anything that is available.

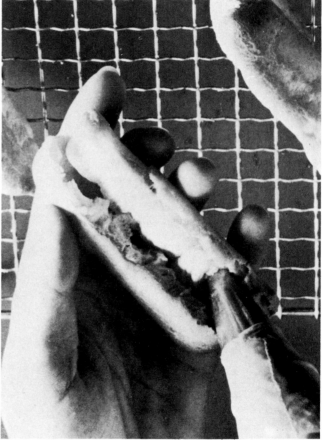

Cassolettes chasseur — Prawn butter balls

4 oz. (8T) butter
2 eggs, beaten
soft white breadcrumbs
oil for deep frying
2 oz. (½ cup) chopped
prawns (shrimp)
3 tablespoons (¼ cup) sauce
béchamel (see recipe page 16)
3 tablespoons (¼ cup) double
(heavy) cream
salt and pepper
extra peeled prawns (shrimp)
fried parsley for garnish

makes 8

Cassolettes used to be small batter cases needing a special mould to make them. These butter ball cases are equally light and crisp and need a great deal of care in the making.

Divide the butter into 8 equal pieces and shape each one into a ball. Place the balls in a bowl of iced water or in the refrigerator until they are very hard. Drain the butter balls well, dip them into the beaten egg and then coat in breadcrumbs. Press the crumbs on well. Repeat this process 3 more times. Continue until all the balls are thickly coated.
Heat the oil for deep frying until 375 °F. (a ¼ inch dice of bread will brown in less than a minute). With a small cutter (a plain icing pipe is good) cut a small round in the breadcrumb coating. Deep fry the butter balls until golden brown and crisp. Cool slightly, then remove the round 'lid' with the point of a knife and tip out the melted butter. Drain well on absorbent kitchen paper and keep hot. Mix the chopped prawns (shrimp) with the sauce béchamel and cream, season to taste, reheat gently without boiling.
Spoon the filling into the prepared cases and arrange the extra whole prawns on the top. Serve immediately on a heated serving plate, garnished with fried parsley.

Croustades de merluche fumée — Smoked haddock in crusty cases

1 sandwich loaf
2 eggs, beaten
fresh white breadcrumbs
oil for deep frying
4 oz. (1 cup) flaked cooked
smoked haddock
4 anchovies, chopped
1 oz. (2T) butter, melted
cayenne pepper
3 tablespoons (¼ cup) double
(heavy) cream

makes 12

Cut the bread into 6 slices, each 1½ inches thick. Cut out 2 rounds from each slice using a biscuit cutter. Dip each round into the beaten egg and then coat in breadcrumbs, pressing them on firmly. Mark another round with a smaller biscuit cutter on the top of each piece of bread.
Heat the oil for deep frying until 375°F. (a ¼ inch dice of bread will brown in less than a minute). Fry the bread rounds until crisp and golden. Carefully remove the smaller round on the top when cooled slightly. Scoop out the soft bread from the centre of the case. Drain on absorbent kitchen paper and keep hot.
Mix the smoked haddock with the anchovies, melted butter, a pinch of cayenne pepper and the cream, in a small saucepan. Reheat without boiling.
Fill the crispy bread cases with the smoked haddock mixture, replacing the lids.
Serve very hot.

Jambon à la diable — Devilled ham

12 rounds cooked ham (2 inches
in diameter)
2 teaspoons French mustard
1 teaspoon English mustard
2 teaspoons chutney
salt
lemon juice
olive oil
6 button mushrooms
½ oz. (1T) butter
6 rounds buttered toast (2
inches diameter)
paprika pepper for garnish
makes 6

Cut the rounds of ham carefully. Mix together the mustards and chutney with salt to taste and a few drops of lemon juice to moisten. Sandwich the ham rounds together in pairs. Brush with olive oil and grill until very hot, 2–3 minutes.
Wipe the mushrooms. Heat the butter in a small frying pan and fry the mushrooms until tender.
Place the ham on to the freshly made hot buttered toast rounds, top with a mushroom. Sprinkle with paprika pepper.
Serve piping hot.

Desserts

At one time the dessert course at a French dinner party
was divided into two parts: first a rich, usually cream,
dessert was served. This was called the 'entremet sucre'
and was followed by a lighter course of either fresh fruit
or cooked fruit.

Fresh fruit is eaten more frequently today than it used to
be, not only because it is very easy to prepare and serve
but because, with a shrinking world, a greater variety of
fruits are available from other countries. Whether serving
local or foreign fruits, always make sure that they are
perfect and unblemished. Wash each piece of fruit
carefully under running cold water and pat it dry with a
clean tea towel or absorbent kitchen paper. Pile the
different fruits in one bowl, making an attractive
arrangement.

Before any sweet course is served, clear the table of the
main course and remove the salt and pepper and bread
and butter, leaving only spoons and forks for a prepared
dessert and small silver knives and forks for the fresh
fruit. Provide small plates.

Sorbet de yaourt à l'orange
Yoghourt orange sorbet

2 × 5 oz. cartons natural yoghourt
1 × 6¼ oz. can concentrated orange juice
grated rind from 2 oranges
sugar to taste
½ oz. (1½ tablespoons) gelatine
2 egg whites
2 oranges
sprigs of mint for decoration
serves 4–6

Although sorbets can be served as a dessert, their place on a French formal dinner menu comes after the relevé (or joint) to clear the palate ready for the roast poultry or game.

Yoghourt is much used in French cookery, especially in the Haute Savoie district where it is made commercially in large amounts.

Turn the refrigerator setting to its lowest point.

Mix the yoghourt, orange juice and grated rind together in a mixing bowl with sugar to taste. Heat 3 tablespoons (¼ cup) water until hot, shower in the gelatine and stir until dissolved. Cool slightly, then add to the yoghourt mixture. Mix well, then put aside until syrupy and beginning to set.

Whisk the egg whites until just stiff, then fold into the yoghourt mixture.

Pour the mixture into a dish or cake tin and freeze until firm.

Peel the oranges, removing all the pith. Slice thinly and remove the pips.

To serve, place layers of orange slices alternately with frozen sorbet. Decorate with sprigs of mint. For a spectacular dessert, try serving the sorbet frozen into half a hollowed out melon.

Yoghourt orange sorbet

Chocolate mousse

Mousse au chocolat
Chocolate mousse

4 oz. plain dark chocolate
4 eggs, separated
double (heavy) cream for decoration

serves 4

Break the chocolate into small pieces and put into a small heatproof bowl with 4 teaspoons water. Place over hot water until the chocolate has melted, stirring until smooth.

Add the egg yolks to the chocolate, stir well and leave until cool. Whisk the egg whites until stiff enough to stand in peaks, then fold into the chocolate mixture. Make sure the mixture is perfectly smooth. Pour the mousse into 4 individual serving dishes and leave until set. Decorate with small rosettes of whipped cream.

Flan au chocolat   Chocolate flan

6 oz. pâte brisée (see recipe)
page 119)
4 oz. dark plain chocolate
3 eggs, separated
¼ pint (⅝ cup) double
(heavy) cream
extra 1 oz. dark plain chocolate
for decoration

Make the pâté brisée. Roll it out on a lightly floured board until it is a thin round, large enough to line an 8 inch diameter flan ring (standing on a baking tray) or a shallow cake tin. Lift the pastry on to the rolling pin and line the flan ring, trim off the excess pastry. Place a piece of greased greaseproof paper on the pastry, fill with baking beans and bake the flan case 'blind' in a moderately hot oven (375°F. Mark 5) for 15 minutes, then remove the paper and beans and continue baking for a further 10–15 minutes or until cooked. Cool on a wire rack.

Break the chocolate into small pieces, place in a heatproof bowl and melt it over a saucepan of hot water. Stir the chocolate until it is melted, taking care that it doesn't become overheated. Beat in the egg yolks, add the brandy, then allow the mixture to cool. Whisk the egg whites until stiff enough to stand in peaks. Fold the whites gently into the chocolate mixture. Pour into the prepared flan case and leave in a cool place until set.

Whip the cream until thickened and spread it over the chocolate filling. Grate the extra chocolate over the top for decoration. Serve as soon as possible.

serves 6

Chocolate flan

Omelette soufflé   Soufflé omelette

3 oz. (scant ½ cup) castor
(superfine) sugar
3 egg yolks
¼ teaspoon vanilla, almond,
lemon or other essence or
1 tablespoon liqueur
6 egg whites
pinch of salt

Soufflé omelettes are usually cooked in the oven in France although they can also be cooked on the hob (on a warming slate in the fireplace) and the top browned under a hot grill.

Put 2 oz. (good ¼ cup) castor (superfine) sugar in a bowl, add the egg yolks and beat thoroughly with a wooden spoon until creamy. Stir in the chosen flavouring.
Whisk the egg whites with salt until stiff enough to stand in peaks, stir 1 tablespoon into the yolk mixture, then carefully fold in the remainder.
Grease an ovenproof dish and pour in the omelette mixture. Pile the egg high and cut some slashes in the sides to help the middle to cook. Bake in a moderate oven (350°F. Mark 4) for 15–20 minutes. Sprinkle the remaining sugar on the top and brown under a very hot grill.

serves 6   Serve immediately.

Apricot soufflé omelette

Omelette soufflée aux abricots
Apricot soufflé omelette

2 eggs, separated
1 tablespoon (1¼T) castor (superfine) sugar
½ oz. (1T) butter
6 oz. hot cooked or canned apricot halves
extra castor sugar

Place the egg yolks in a mixing bowl, add the sugar and 2 teaspoons water. Beat with a wooden spoon until creamy. Whisk the egg whites until stiff enough to stand in peaks. Fold the whites gently into the creamed yolks.

Heat the butter in a 6–7 inch omelette pan until very hot. Add the egg and cook until it is golden brown underneath. Put the pan under a hot grill and lightly brown the top of the omelette. Slide the omelette on to a heated serving plate, place the hot apricots on top of half the omelette. Fold over the other half and dust the top with the extra castor sugar.

serves 1–2   Serve immediately.

Chartreuse de fraises
Strawberry Chartreuse

1 pint (2½ cups) lemon jelly (jello)
24 small strawberries angelica
¼ pint (⅝ cup) double (heavy) cream

Use freshly made lemon jelly (jello) which is cool but not set. Pour a little (about 2–3 tablespoons (scant ¼ cup)) into the bottom of a 1 pint (2½ cups) capacity deep jelly mould. Rotate the mould until the whole of the inside is covered with a set layer of jelly (jello). It is helpful in setting this layer if the mould is very cold and standing in a bowl of crushed ice.

Pour in more jelly (jello) to ½ inch depth and allow to set. Place 8 small strawberries on the jelly (jello) and use small pieces of angelica to form the 'stalks'. Pour in more jelly (jello) to cover the strawberries well. Allow to set, then add another layer of strawberries and angelia, covering with more jelly (jello). Allow to set, then arrange the remaining strawberries on top. Cover with the remaining jelly (jello) and put aside in a cool place until the entire mould is firmly set.

Turn out of the mould on to a wet serving plate just before serving. Decorate with rosettes of whipped cream. Dry the plate before serving.

note: other fruit—bananas, mandarin orange segments, pineapple

serves 4–6   chunks and so on—can be used in this manner.

104

Bavaroise à l'orange
Orange cream

¼ pint (⅝ cup) milk
1 egg
1 egg yolk
¼ pint (⅝ cup) orange juice
juice of ½ lemon
½ oz. (1½ tablespoons) gelatine
2 oz. (¼ cup) castor
(superfine) sugar
¼ pint (⅝ cup) double or
heavy cream
extra double (heavy) cream for
decoration

Place the milk in a bowl, add the egg and egg yolk and whisk lightly. Place the bowl over a small saucepan of simmering water (don't allow the bowl to touch the water). Cook gently, stirring occasionally with a wooden spoon, until the custard is thick enough to coat the back of the spoon.
Mix orange and lemon juice together.
Dissolve the gelatine in 3 tablespoons (¼ cup) hot water. Add the sugar, the dissolved gelatine and fruit juices to the cooked custard. Strain, then put aside until cold.
Whip the cream until thickened but not stiff. Fold the cream carefully into the gelatine mixture then cool until it begins to thicken.
When the cream is thickened, pour it into an oiled 1 pint (2½ cups) mould to set.

serves 4

Turn the cream out of the mould on to a serving plate. Decorate with rosettes of stiffly whipped cream.

Bavaroise à l'abricot
Apricot cream

Use ¼ pint (⅝ cup) apricot purée instead of orange juice and only use ¼ oz. (¾ tablespoon) gelatine.

Bavaroise au rhum
Rum cream

Use ¾ pint (⅝ cup) extra milk instead of the orange and lemon juice. Add 1–2 tablespoons rum.

Bavaroise rubané à trois parfums
Ribbon cream

Make the cream as for Bavaroise au Rhum, omitting the rum.
Divide the mixture into three bowls. Add ½ teaspoon coffee essence to one bowl; a few drops of vanilla essence to the second; a few drops of almond essence with a little green colouring, to the third. Pour the first mixture into the oiled mould and allow to set. Pour the second mixture on top and when this is set pour on the third mixture.
Unmould when all three layers are well set.

Crème brûlée
Scorched cream

½ pint (1¼ cups) double
(heavy) cream
4 egg yolks, beaten
3 tablespoons (¼ cup) icing
(confectionery) sugar
½ teaspoon vanilla essence
castor (superfine) sugar

Pour the cream into the top of a double saucepan (or a small heatproof bowl) and place it over hot water. When hot, pour the cream on to the egg yolks, beating constantly.
Return the mixture to the saucepan, add the icing (confectionery) sugar and vanilla essence and cook over hot water until the mixture thickens, stirring constantly.
Pour custard into a 1 pint (2¼ cups) capacity ovenproof dish. Chill overnight.
Sprinkle the top of the custard liberally with castor (superfine) sugar 2–3 hours before serving. Cook under a hot grill until the sugar has caramelized to a deep golden brown. Chill again before serving.

serves 4

note: although this is delicious on its own, it can be served with fresh or stewed fruit to make a more substantial dessert.

Charlotte russe
Bavarian cream and jelly with sponge fingers

½ pint (1¼ cups) jelly (jello)
(use lemon or a flavour which
will blend with the cream filling)
about 12 sponge fingers
baverois cream (see recipe
page 105)
double (heavy) cream for
decoration

serves 4

This dessert takes its name from the mould in which it is made. A
charlotte mould is round and has slightly sloping plain sides.

Pour the cooled, unset, jelly (jello) into the bottom of a 1 pint (2½
cups) charlotte mould to ½ inch depth.
Cut the sponge fingers to the height of the sides of the mould (less
½ inch) and arrange them around the edge, rounded ends downwards
on the jelly (jello). The fingers should fit tightly, leaving as little
space as possible between them. Pour the baverois cream into the
mould and put in a cool place to set.
Turn the charlotte russe out of the mould on to a wet serving plate
(this helps if you have to move the cream into position). The
remaining jelly (jello) will now have set, so chop it coarsely with a
wet knife and arrange it around the charlotte russe.
Decorate with rosettes of whipped cream. Serve as soon as possible.

Crème caramel
Cream caramel

2 oz. (¼ cup) granulated
(crystal) sugar
3 tablespoons (¼ cup) water
2 eggs
2 egg yolks
¾ pint (approx. 2 cups) milk
1 oz. (2 tablespoons) castor
(superfine) sugar
few drops vanilla essence

serves 4–6

Place the granulated (crystal) sugar in a small saucepan with 2
tablespoons of the water. Heat gently, stirring, until the sugar is
dissolved. Boil briskly until the syrup is golden brown (do not stir).
Remove from the heat and add the remaining 1 tablespoon of water,
stirring until the caramel and water have combined. Pour into a
warm, dry 1 pint (2½ cups) capacity heatproof dish. Make sure that
the base of the dish is completely covered with the caramel.
Put the eggs, egg yolks, milk and castor (superfine) sugar into a
mould. Mix thoroughly but do not let the mixture become frothy.
Strain the egg custard into the dish on top of the caramel. Place the
mould inside a dish or roasting pan, adding enough water to come
halfway up the side of the egg custard mould. Cook in a moderately
slow oven (325°F. Mark 3) for about 50 minutes or until firm and set.
Allow to cool.
Chill, then turn out of the mould on to a serving plate and serve as
soon as possible.

note: this recipe can also be cooked in individual dariole moulds.
Divide the caramel and then the custard equally between 6 moulds
and cook them for 25–30 minutes.

Cream caramel

106

Oeufs à la neige   Snow eggs

3 eggs, separated
4 oz. (good ½ cup) castor (superfine) sugar
¾ pint (scant 2 cups) milk
½ teaspoon finely grated lemon peel

serves 4

Whisk the egg whites until standing in stiff peaks. Add 3 tablespoons (¼ cup) castor (superfine) sugar and continue whisking until the mixture is firm and glossy.

Place the milk in a large saucepan and heat it until bubbles begin to rise to the surface (do not allow it to boil). Place tablespoonfuls of the mixture into the milk and poach them gently for 5 minutes, turning once. Carefully remove the cooked egg white from the milk with a slotted spoon and drain well on absorbent kitchen paper. When all the egg white has been cooked, strain the milk.

Place the egg yolks in the top of a double saucepan (or in a heatproof bowl) over gently simmering water. Add the milk and beat lightly. Add the remaining sugar and cook, stirring constantly, until the custard thickens and coats the back of the spoon. Add the lemon rind. Pour the custard into a serving bowl and arrange the poached egg whites on top.

Chill before serving.

note: for a more spectacular dessert, pour caramel over the egg whites and scatter flaked almonds on top. To make the caramel, place 3 tablespoons (¼ cup) castor sugar in a small heavy saucepan. Heat very gently until the sugar is melted and golden.

Charlotte russe

Crêpes suzette · Curaçao and tangerine pancakes

8 cooked crêpes (see recipe
page 40)
2 lumps sugar
2 tangerines
1 oz. (2T) butter
1 oz. (2 tablespoons) castor
(superfine) sugar
1 tablespoon curaçao
3 tablespoons (¼ cup) rum

Prepare the crêpes.
Rub the lumps of sugar all over the unpeeled tangerines until they
are saturated in tangerine oil and zest. Crush the lumps of sugar in a
mixing bowl and beat in the butter. Add the castor (superfine) sugar,
curaçao and 1 tablespoon of juice squeezed from the tangerines. Mix
thoroughly.
Reheat the crêpes, covered in aluminium foil, in a moderate oven
(350°F. Mark 4) for 15 minutes. Spread the hot crêpes with tangerine
butter and fold each in four. Place them in a heated, flameproof
serving dish. Heat the rum gently in a small saucepan until warmed,
then ignite and pour over the crêpes. Serve immediately.

serves 4

note: use oranges if tangerines are not available.

Riz à l'impératrice · Empress rice

4 oz. (½ cup) round grain rice
1 pint (2½ cups) milk
¼ teaspoon vanilla essence
4 oz. (½ cup) granulated
(crystal) sugar
1 oz. (2T) butter
4 oz. glacé (candied) fruits
3 tablespoons (¼ cup) kirsch
½ pint (1¼ cups) double
(heavy) cream
4 egg yolks, lightly beaten
2 oz. (¼ cup) granulated
(crystal) sugar
extra ½ pint (1¼ cups) milk
½ oz. (1½ tablespoons) gelatine
fruit sauce (see recipe
page 22), optional

This dish may be served on its own or it can be decorated with fresh
fruit. Try it served with pears, peeled, cored and halved.

Lightly grease a 2½–3 pint (6¼–7½ cups) capacity decorative mould or
charlotte tin.
Put the rice in a saucepan and cover with water. Bring to the boil,
simmer 2–3 minutes and drain the rice. Return the rice to the
saucepan, add the milk and vanilla essence, bring to the boil and
simmer, covered, stirring occasionally, until the rice is tender and
the milk absorbed. Stir in 2 oz. of the sugar and butter. Allow the
rice to cool.
Chop the glacé (candied) fruit into small pieces and soak them in
kirsch. Whip the cream until stiff and fold into the rice.
Mix the egg yolks and remaining 2 oz. sugar together in a bowl. Put
the extra milk into a saucepan and heat it until bubbles begin to rise
to the surface (do not allow it to boil). Pour the milk on to the
egg yolks, add the gelatine and stir until the gelatine is dissolved.
Cool. Strain the custard on to the rice, add the soaked glacé (candied)
fruits and stir together well. Spoon the prepared mixture into the
greased mould. Put in a cool place, preferably the refrigerator, until
set.
Turn out of the mould on to a chilled serving plate and serve
decorated with fruit or with a fruit sauce.

serves 4–6

Crêpes suzette

Coeur à la crème   Cream hearts

8 oz. cottage cheese
½ pint (1¼ cups) double (heavy) cream
2 level teaspoons (scant ¼ cup) sifted icing (confectionery) sugar
8 oz. strawberries, hulled
1 teaspoon lemon juice
2 tablespoons (scant ¼ cup) castor (superfine) sugar

Coeur à la Crème is a traditional French sweet. It is very rich and delicious when served with soft fruits such as strawberries, raspberries, peaches and fresh currants. It is customary to set the cream in special heart-shaped moulds with perforated bases. It can, however, be made with equal success in a muslin-lined bowl-shaped sieve.

Rub the cottage cheese through a sieve into a mixing bowl. Stir in the cream and icing (confectionery) sugar and beat well. Either press the cottage cheese mixture into 6 individual coeur à la crème moulds or in a muslin lined sieve. Allow to drain overnight.
Turn the cream out of the mould on to a serving plate. Sprinkle the strawberries with lemon juice and castor (superfine) sugar and arrange them around the coeur à la crème.
Serve as soon as possible.

Cream hearts   serves 6   **note**: macaroons (see recipe page 126) are good served with this dish.

Crêpes aux framboises Raspberry pancakes

8 cooked crêpes (see recipe page 40)	Prepare the crêpes and keep them hot.
1×12 oz. packet frozen or canned raspberries	Defrost the frozen raspberries or drain them if canned.
1 oz. (2 tablespoons) granulated (crystal) sugar	Reserve the liquid and make up to ½ pint (1¼ cups) with water. Place the liquid with the sugar in a saucepan, heat, stirring to boiling point. Blend the cornflour (cornstarch) with a little more water in a
1 tablespoon (1½ tablespoons) cornflour (cornstarch)	bowl and pour the boiling liquid on to it, stirring constantly, then return to the saucepan, bring to the boil and simmer 2–3 minutes
red food colouring	until thick.
double (heavy) cream for serving	Add red food colouring if necessary.
	Fold each crêpe in half, place some of the raspberry mixture on to the centre of each. Fold the sides of the crêpe in so that the raspberries still show.
serves 4	Serve as soon as possible with a bowl of whipped cream.

Poires belle Hélène Pears with ice cream and chocolate sauce

8 oz. (1 cup) granulated (crystal) sugar	Place the sugar in a saucepan with ½ pint (1¼ cups) water and heat gently, stirring until the sugar is dissolved. Stir in the honey.
3 tablespoons (¼ cup) honey	Peel core and halve the pears. Cook the halves gently in the prepared
4 pears	syrup for 15–20 minutes or until tender. Drain and cool.
vanilla ice cream	Place a portion of ice cream in the base of each of 4 individual
½ pint (1¼ cups) sauce chocolat (see recipe page 22)	serving glasses. Arrange the pears on top. Chill the sauce chocolat and pour over the pears. Serve immediately.
serves 4	

Poires bourguignonne Burgundy pears

4 pears	Peel the pears, without removing the stalks. Place the sugar in a
8 oz. (1 cup) granulated (crystal) sugar	saucepan with ¼ pint (⅝ cup) water.
¼ pint (⅝ cup) red Burgundy wine	Bring to the boil, stirring until the sugar has dissolved. Add the pears and simmer, covered, for 15 minutes. Add the Burgundy and
red food colouring (optional)	continue cooking for a further 15 minutes, uncovered. Add a little red food colouring if liked.
	Remove and drain the pears, allowing them to cool. Bring the syrup to the boil again and cook rapidly, stirring, until thick. Pour over the pears, cool and chill.
	note: apples can also be prepared in this way. A mixture of both
serves 4	pears and apples can make an interesting dessert.

Pêches au miel Honeyed peaches

6 fresh peaches	Skin the peaches by first plunging them into boiling water for 1
1 lemon	minute, then placing them in cold water and peeling off the skin.
rind of 1 orange	Halve the peaches and place each half in lemon juice to prevent
4 oz. (good ¼ cup) honey	discolouration.
	Peel the thin zest off the orange and lemon with a potato peeler. Place these strips in a saucepan with the honey and ¼ pint (⅝ cup) water. Heat the saucepan, gently stirring, until the honey has dissolved, then boil rapidly, uncovered, for 5 minutes.
serves 6	Remove the rinds and pour the syrup over the peaches. Cool, then chill in the refrigerator. Serve with whipped cream.

Honeyed peaches

Soufflé au citron Lemon soufflé

3 eggs, separated
3 oz. (scant ½ cup) castor (superfine) sugar
2 lemons
scant ½ oz. (1½ tablespoons) gelatine
¼ pint (⅝ cup) double (heavy) cream
extra double (heavy) cream and chopped nuts for decoration

Lightly grease a 1 pint (2½ cups) capacity soufflé dish. Cut a double strip of greaseproof paper the height of the dish plus 3 inches and long enough to go around it. Grease the top 3 inches and tie the paper, greased side inside, around the dish.
Place the egg yolks, castor (superfine) sugar, juice and finely grated lemon rind in a heatproof mixing bowl. Put the bowl over a pan of hot water and whisk until the mixture is thickened and creamy. Remove from the heat and whisk until cooled. Dissolve the gelatine in 3 tablespoons (¼ cup) hot water and whisk into the egg mixture. Half whip the cream and fold it into the egg mixture. Cool.
Whisk the egg whites until stiff enough to stand in peaks. When the cream mixture is just about to set, fold in the egg whites. Pour into the prepared soufflé dish and put in a cool place to set firmly. Remove the greaseproof paper from the soufflé, carefully easing it away from soufflé with the back of a knife. Decorate with chopped nuts pressed around the sides and rosettes of whipped cream on top.

serves 5–6 Serve as soon as possible.

Soufflé aux abricots Apricot soufflé

Omit the lemon rind and juice from the above recipe. Use instead ¼ pint (⅝ cup) apricot purée and the juice of ½ a lemon. Cook the egg yolks and sugar and, when cooled, add the purée and juice.

Soufflé aux fraises Strawberry soufflé

Prepare the soufflé as for soufflé aux abricots, substituting strawberry purée for the apricot and omitting the lemon juice.

Lemon soufflé

Pommes en charlotte Apple charlotte

½ large sandwich loaf, thick sliced
6 oz. (12T) unsalted butter
6 tablespoons (½ cup) oil
3½ lbs. cooking apples, peeled, cored and sliced
1 oz. (2T) butter
juice of 1 lemon
¼ teaspoon ground cinnamon
4 oz. (½ cup) granulated (crystal) sugar
6 tablespoons (½ cup) apricot jam

serves 4–6

Grease a 3 pint (7½ cups) capacity charlotte mould with butter. Removing the crusts from the slices of bread, cut out 6–8 heart shaped croûtes with a biscuit cutter. Cut the remaining slices into 'fingers' about ½–¾ inch wide and slightly longer than the depth of the charlotte mould. Heat the unsalted butter and the oil together in a large frying pan. Fry the hearts and fingers of bread until golden. Arrange the hearts, overlapping, in the base of the charlotte mould. Stand the fingers of bread around the sides, again overlapping. Prepare the apples. Melt the butter in a large saucepan. Add the lemon juice, cinnamon and apples. Cover the pan and cook very gently until the apples are soft and pulpy. Stir in the sugar and apricot jam until dissolved.

Place the apple pulp in the mould on the fried bread, fill the mould well, as the filling tends to become absorbed during cooking. Cover the apple with more fried bread fingers. Bake in a moderately hot oven (375°F. Mark 5) for 10–15 minutes.

Cool slightly, then turn the apple charlotte out of the mould on to a heated serving plate.

note: this dish can also be served chilled.

Pommes flambées
Flaming apples

8 dessert apples
lemon juice
6 oz. (1 cup) soft brown sugar
1 teaspoon ground cinnamon
6 tablespoons (½ cup) rum

Peel the apples, without removing the stalks. Dip each apple in lemon juice to prevent discolouration.

Place the sugar and cinnamon in a large saucepan with 2 pints (5 cups) water. Bring to the boil, stirring until the sugar has dissolved. Add the apples and simmer, covered, for 10–15 minutes or until just tender. Drain, place on a heatproof serving dish and keep hot.

Boil the cooking syrup fast, uncovered, until it begins to thicken. Pour the syrup, then the rum, over the apples. Ignite and serve immediately.

serves 4

Tarte aux pommes
Apple flan

6 oz. pâte brisée (see recipe page 119)
2 lbs. cooking apples
¼ pint (⅝ cup) white wine
½ lemon
2 oz. (4T) butter
4 oz. (½ cup) granulated (crystal) sugar
4 crisp eating apples
3 tablespoons (¼ cup) apricot jam
double (heavy) cream for serving

A delicious and easy to prepare dish which can be eaten hot or cold. The recipe originated in the Normandy district of France, which is renowned for its orchards.

Make the pâte brisée. Roll it out on a lightly floured board into a thin round, large enough to line an 8 inch diameter flan ring (standing on a baking tray) or a shallow cake tin. Lift the pastry on a rolling pin, line the flan ring and trim off excess pastry. Peel, core and cut the cooking apples into quarters. Place them in a saucepan with the wine, a strip of lemon rind (peel this off with a potato peeler), butter and 2 oz. (¼ cup) sugar. Cover the pan and simmer gently until the apples are very tender. Remove the lemon rind. Purée the apples by pressing through a sieve or in a blender. Place the apple purée in the unbaked flan case. Peel and core the eating apples, then slice thinly. Arrange the slices, overlapping, on top of the purée. Sprinkle with the remaining sugar and bake in a moderately hot oven (375°F. Mark 5) for 25–30 minutes or until the apples are cooked and the pastry is golden.

Meanwhile, heat the apricot jam in a small saucepan with 1 tablespoon lemon juice. Stir until well blended. Sieve.

Glaze the hot cooked flan with apricot glaze. Serve with a bowl of whipped cream.

serves 6

Tarte aux pommes meringue

Prepare the above recipe but omit the eating apples and the glaze. Whisk 2 eggs until stiff enough to stand in firm peaks. Fold in 4 oz. (good ½ cup) castor (superfine) sugar. Pile the meringue on top of the apple purée in the cooked flan, bringing the meringue down to touch the pastry all round. Bake in a moderate oven (350°F. Mark 4) until the meringue is a pale golden, about 10–15 minutes. Decorate with small marzipan apples.

Tarte aux pommes et oranges

Prepare the above recipe but omit the eating apples and the glaze. Slice thinly 2 thin-skinned oranges. Place 4 oz. (½ cup) granulated (crystal) sugar in a saucepan with ¼ pint (⅝ cup) water, bring to the boil, stirring until the sugar is dissolved. Add the orange rounds and carefully poach them until they are tender. Place cooked orange slices on top of the apple purée in the cooked flan. Boil the remaining syrup very rapidly until it is thickening and beginning to caramelize. Glaze the top of the flan. Serve.

Apple and orange flan

1
2 3

4

5

6

7

Cakes and pastries

French pâtisserie is almost legendary. Anyone who has visited France will know the delicious smell that wafts out of the patisserie shops and will no doubt have sampled their wares. Those who live outside France must make their own. Follow the recipes in this chapter carefully; some are very delicate and tricky to make, but with care you will produce a superb result.

Pâtisserie is served as a dessert with coffee, or, in the case of plainer breads such as croissants or brioches, for breakfast. They are fairly time-consuming to make but the extra effort is well worthwhile, particularly for a special occasion. Serve them as fresh as possible.

St. Honoré cake

Pâte brisée — Short crust pastry

8 oz. (2 cups) plain (all purpose) flour
pinch of salt
4 oz. (8T) butter or margarine
1 egg
3 tablespoons ($\frac{1}{4}$ cup) water

Sift the flour on to a cold surface, make a well in the centre and add the salt, chopped butter, egg and water. Work the butter, egg and water together with the fingertips, gradually blending in the flour. Knead lightly until smooth. Cover with aluminium foil or polythene and put in a cool place for 30 minutes. Use as required.

Pâte sucrée — Sweet short crust pastry

8 oz. (2 cups) plain (all purpose) flour
4 oz. (8T) butter or margarine
2 oz. (good $\frac{1}{4}$ cup) castor (superfine) sugar
2 egg yolks
$\frac{1}{4}$ teaspoon vanilla essence
3 tablespoons ($\frac{1}{4}$ cup) water

Sift the flour on to a cold surface and make a well in the centre. Add the butter, (cut into pieces), sugar, egg yolks, vanilla essence and water. Work these ingredients together with the fingertips, gradually blending in the flour. Knead lightly until smooth. Cover with aluminium foil or polythene and put in a cool place for 30 minutes.
Use as required.

Pâte à choux — Choux pastry

4 oz. (8T) butter or margarine
$\frac{1}{2}$ pint (1$\frac{1}{4}$ cups) water
5 oz. (1$\frac{1}{4}$ cups) plain (all purpose) flour
4 eggs, beaten

Placing the butter and water in a saucepan, heat slowly until the butter is melted and the water at boiling point. Remove from the heat. Add all the sifted flour and beat well with a wooden spoon until the mixture is smooth and falls from the sides of the pan. Allow the paste to cool slightly, then gradually add the beaten eggs and mix well.
Use as required.

Pâte feuilletée — Puff pastry

8 oz. (2 cups) plain (all purpose) flour
$\frac{1}{2}$ teaspoon salt
8 oz. ($\frac{1}{2}$ lb.) butter or margarine
scant $\frac{1}{4}$ pint ($\frac{1}{2}$ cup) iced water
1 teaspoon lemon juice

Sift the flour and salt on to a cold surface, make a well in the centre and add 1 oz. of butter, the water and the lemon juice. Using the fingertips, work the ingredients together to make a soft dough. Knead very lightly, put on a plate and cover with aluminium foil or polythene. Leave in a cool place for 30 minutes.
Shape the remaining butter into a rectangle block about 4 × 2 × 1 inch. Roll out the dough to a square about $\frac{1}{4}$ inch thick. Place the butter in the centre and wrap it up like a parcel. Roll the parcel of dough and fat into an oblong about 12 × 5 inches. Mark the dough lightly into thirds with a knife. Fold the top third down over the middle third and then fold up the bottom third. Turn the dough a quarter turn to the left (folds are then to right and left), roll and fold as before. Place the dough on a plate, cover with foil or polythene and rest in a cool place again for 30 minutes.
Roll, fold and turn the dough 4 more times. Leave, as before, for 30 minutes. Roll, fold and turn the dough twice more. Leave for 15 minutes, then use as required.

Pâte genoise — Genoise sponge

4 eggs
4 oz. (good $\frac{1}{2}$ cup) castor (superfine) sugar
3 oz. (6T) unsalted butter or margarine, melted and cooled
3 oz. ($\frac{3}{4}$ cup) plain (all purpose) flour

serves 4–6

Place the eggs and castor (superfine) sugar in a large bowl over a saucepan of simmering water. Whisk the eggs and sugar together until the mixture is light in colour and thick enough to leave a trail. Remove the bowl from the heat and whisk for a further 3–4 minutes. Add half the butter then half the sifted flour and fold them into the egg mixture using a metal spoon. Fold in the remaining butter and flour. Mix gently until smooth.
Use as required. (See overleaf for ideas on using pâte genoise.)

Using pâte genoise

Pâte genoise can be cooked in a deep 7 inch diameter cake tin or in two shallow 7 inch diameter tins. For a slab cake, use an 8 by 12 inch rectangular cake tin. Bake in a moderate oven (350°F. Mark 4) for 25–40 minutes, according to the tin used.

Pâte genoise can then be decorated in a variety of ways. Recipes are given for the elaborate gâteaux but an ordinary sponge can be effectively decorated with the minimum of ingredients.

Whipped cream makes an easy and delicious filling for two cakes sandwiched together and it needs only a little more on top, decorated with flaked toasted almonds, for a really luscious gâteau. Try this with pâte genoise au chocolat (below).

Alternatively, bake the entire mixture in a deep cake tin and, when cool, spread the sides with cream and press flaked toasted almonds or toasted desiccated coconut on to the cream with a palate knife. Pipe extra cream on top and your gâteau will have a very professional finish.

Another spectacular idea is to bake the pâte genoise in one 8 inch diameter shallow tin and one 6 inch diameter shallow tin. Sandwich the two cooled cakes together with a little whipped cream and pile fresh seasoned fruit on top. Finish off the gâteau by glazing the fruit with a little syrup thickened with arrowroot and boiled until clear (1 teaspoon arrowroot to $\frac{1}{2}$ tablespoon sugar dissolved in $\frac{1}{4}$ pint ($\frac{5}{8}$ cup) water and cooled). Spread extra whipped cream around the sides and press on chopped almonds. Pipe rosettes of cream around the top.

Pâte genoise au chocolat Chocolate Genoise sponge

Make the recipe as given above but use 2 oz. ($\frac{1}{2}$ cup) plain (all purpose) flour with 1 oz. ($\frac{1}{4}$ cup) cocoa sifted together instead of 3 oz. ($\frac{3}{4}$ cup) plain (all purpose) flour.

Genoise sponge (below)   *Peach cake (right)*

Gâteau aux amandes   Almond cake

1 quantity pâte genoise
few drops of almond essence
4 egg whites
6 oz. (scant 1 cup) castor
(superfine) sugar
2 oz. (½ cup) flaked almonds
1 oz. (2 tablespoons) granulated
(crystal) sugar
¼ pint (⅝ cup) double
(heavy) cream

serves 8

Grease and flour two 8 inch diameter sandwich tins, preferably with removable bases. Make the pâte genoise and fold in the almond essence and melted butter. Pour the mixture into the tins, dividing it equally between the two.
Whisk the egg whites until stiff, add half the castor (superfine) sugar and continue whisking until stiff again. Fold in the remaining castor sugar with a metal spoon. Spread the meringue on top of the pâte genoise, dividing it equally between the two tins. Mix the flaked almonds with granulated (crystal) sugar and sprinkle over both meringues. Bake in a moderate oven (350°F. Mark 4) for 40–45 minutes. Allow the cake to cool in the tins before removing. Whip the cream until stiff and sandwich the two cakes together.

Gâteau au chocolat   Chocolate cake

1 quantity pâte genoise au
chocolat (see recipe page 120)
3 oz. (⅜ cup) granulated
(crystal) sugar
3 oz. (6T) butter or margarine
3 tablespoons (¼ cup) milk
8 oz. (1¾ cups) sifted icing
(confectionery) sugar
1½ tablespoons cocoa
4 oz. plain dark chocolate

serves 8

Grease and line the bases of two 7 inch diameter sandwich tins with greased greaseproof paper. Make the pâte genoise au chocolat and pour it carefully into the tins, dividing the mixture equally.
Bake in a moderate oven (350°F. Mark 4) for 20–25 minutes or until firm and just cooked. Cool on a wire rack.
Place the granulated (crystal) sugar in a saucepan with butter or margarine and the milk. Heat gently, stirring until the sugar is dissolved and the mixture boiling. Boil for 1 minute. Cool quickly by standing the saucepan in a bowl of cold water. Stir occasionally. Sift the icing (confectionery) sugar and cocoa together and add them to the cooled syrup, beating well until thick and fluffy.
Cut the cold cakes in half and sandwich the layers together again with a quarter of the chocolate icing between each layer. Spread the remaining quarter around the sides.
Break the chocolate into small pieces and melt in a bowl over hot water. Spread half over the top of the cake. Spread the remainder on to a plate or a piece of aluminium foil and allow to harden. Cut this into squares and decorate the sides of the cake.

Gâteau aux pêches   Peach cake

1 quantity pâte genoise (see
recipe page 119)
3 tablespoons (¼ cup) peach or
apricot jam
¼ pint (⅝ cup) double
(heavy) cream
13 sponge fingers
4 peaches or 1×15½ oz. can
peach halves
1 teaspoon sugar (optional)
1 teaspoon arrowroot

serves 8

Grease and flour two 7 inch diameter sandwich tins. Make the pâte genoise and pour it carefully into the tins, dividing the mixture equally. Bake in a moderate oven (350°F. Mark 4) for 20–25 minutes or until firm and just cooked. Cool on a wire rack.
Spread one of the cakes with peach or apricot jam and place the other cake on top. Whip the cream until stiff. Cut the sponge fingers in half and arrange the halves around the sandwiched cake, spreading each one with a little whipped cream to make them stick. If fresh peaches are being used, first skin them by plunging them into boiling water for 1 minute, then rinsing them in cold water and peeling off the skin. Cut the peaches in half and remove the stones. Drain canned peach halves, if used, and reserve the syrup. Measure ¼ pint (⅝ cup) peach syrup or measure ¼ pint (⅝ cup) water and add the sugar. Blend a little of the liquid with the arrowroot in a bowl, place the remainder in a saucepan and heat until boiling. Add all the liquid to the arrowroot in the bowl, then return to the pan and bring to the boil, stirring until it clears. Cool.
Arrange the peach halves on top of the gâteau and spoon a little of the arrowroot mixture over them to glaze. When the glaze is completely cold, pipe rosettes of the remaining cream between the peaches. A ribbon can be tied around the biscuits for a very decorative finish.
Serve as soon as possible.

Gâteau surprise
Surprise cake

1 quantity pâte genoise (see recipe page 119)
¼ pint (⅝ cup) double (heavy) cream
6 tablespoons (½ cup) mixed fruit salad
castor sugar
3 oz. (½ cup) icing (confectionery) sugar
apricot jam
2 oz. (½ cup) chopped almonds
glacé (candied) fruits for decoration
serves 8

Grease and flour a 7 inch diameter deep cake tin. Make the pâte genoise, pour gently into the tin and bake in a moderate oven (350°F. Mark 4) for 35–40 minutes or until firm. Cool on a wire rack. Whip the cream until thick, mix with the fruit salad and add castor sugar to taste. Cut out a lid from the sponge, allowing a ½–¾ inch border. Hollow out the centre of the sponge with a spoon. Fill the space with the fruit and cream. Replace the lid.
Mix the sifted icing (confectionery) sugar with enough water to make a thick glacé icing. Warm the apricot jam slightly and brush the edges of the sponge generously, using a palette knife dipped in the jam, then press chopped nuts firmly on to the jam coating. Pour the icing on to the top of the sponge, hiding the joins of the lid. Decorate with glacé (candied) fruits and serve as soon as possible.

Tonille aux ananas
Pineapple nut shortcake

4 oz. (good 1 cup) castor (superfine) sugar
6 oz. (12T) butter
6 oz. (1½ cups) freshly ground toasted hazelnuts
8 oz. (2 cups) plain (all purpose) flour
pinch of salt
½ pint (1¼ cups) double (heavy) cream
2×15½ oz. cans pineapple rings
1 tablespoon icing (confectionery) sugar
extra icing sugar for decoration

serves 6–8

Cream the butter and sugar together in a mixing bowl until soft and fluffy. Add the hazelnuts and mix well. Sift the flour and salt together and work into the butter mixture. Knead lightly. Divide the dough into three pieces and roll two pieces into 8–9 inch diameter rounds, and one 7 inch round on a lightly floured board. Allow to rest in a cool place for 10–20 minutes. Place the rounds on a lightly greased baking tray and bake in a moderately hot oven (375°F. Mark 5) for about 8 minutes. Cool slightly before removing them from the tray. Cut the smaller one into eighths while still warm. Drain the pineapple. Whip the cream until stiff and fold in 1 tablespoon [1¼T] pineapple syrup and the icing (confectionery) sugar. Place a biscuit round on a serving plate, spread it with half of the cream and arrange 4 of the pineapple rings on top. Place another biscuit round on the pineapple and spread with the remaining cream. Arrange the eighths of biscuit like the spokes of a wheel, at an angle, in the cream. Cut the remaining pineapple rings in halves and arrange them between the biscuit wedges.
Serve as soon as possible, dusted with sifted icing sugar.

Chantilly feuilles
Chantilly cream with crisp nut leaves

5 egg whites
2 oz. (½ cup) ground hazelnuts
2 oz. (½ cup) ground walnuts
5 oz. (¾ cup) castor (superfine) sugar
2 oz. (½ cup) plain (all purpose) flour
2 oz. (4T) butter, melted
vanilla essence
1½ oz. dark plain chocolate
½ pint (1¼ cups) double (heavy) cream
1 lb. ripe pears or other fruit (apricots, peaches, strawberries, raspberries etc., as available)
icing sugar

Place 4 of the egg whites in a bowl and whisk until they are stiff enough to stand in peaks. Stir in the hazelnuts, walnuts, castor (superfine) sugar, flour, melted butter and a few drops of vanilla essence, blending gently but thoroughly. Grease 4 baking trays lightly and mark a 6-inch circle on each. Divide the meringue mixture between the 4 circles and spread evenly to form rounds. Bake in a moderate oven (350°F. Mark 4) for about 30 minutes or until the rounds are a pale golden brown in colour. Trim, remove from the baking trays and cool on a wire rack.
Place the chopped chocolate in a heatproof bowl over a saucepan of hot water, until melted. Mix with a palette knife until smooth. Spread the chocolate on waxed paper and allow to set. Cut into rounds 1½ inches in diameter. Cut each round in half to make semi-circles. Whip the cream with a few drops of vanilla essence, until stiff. Whisk the remaining egg white until stiff, then fold into the cream. Prepare the fruit, skin if necessary and remove pips or stones, then chop them and mix into the cream.
Place one layer round on a serving plate, spread it with a quarter of the cream and fruit. Top with another round and continue until all the rounds are sandwiched. Spread the top with cream and decorate with the chocolate. Serve as soon as possible.

123

Petit fours

1 quantity pâte genoise (see recipe page 119), 1 day old. Make it in a greased and floured 8×12 inch shallow cake tin. Bake it in a moderate oven (350° Mark 4) for 25–30 minutes.
Apricot jam, warmed and sieved.
Almond paste. Make this by mixing 4 oz. (1 cup) ground almonds with 2 oz. ($\frac{2}{3}$ cup) icing (confectionery) sugar (sieved). Mix to a firm paste with a little egg white
Finely chopped almonds.
Glacé icing. Icing (confectionery) sugar, sieved and mixed with enough water to give a good coating consistency. (Cover this icing with a damp cloth).
Butter icing. Use 2 oz. (4T) butter creamed with 4 oz. (1$\frac{1}{3}$ cups) sifted icing (confectionery) sugar.
Food colourings.
Decorations. Crystallized flowers, glacé fruits, mimosa balls, silver dragees.

Pineapple nut shortcake (below)

Chantilly cream with crisp nut leaves (top right)

Fruit pastries (below right)

Petit fours are small, rich fancy cakes served in France for afternoon tea, parties (such as an engagement, wedding, christening etc. . . .), accompanying after dinner coffee or even with ice cream.
They should be very small, two or three mouthfuls at the most, and should be neat, smooth and delicately coloured with an appropriate and, where possible, original decoration.
Petit fours riche are made from pâte genoise (see recipe page 119). It is best if the sponge is made the day before it is needed as it will then be firmer and less likely to crumble.
Before starting to decorate the petit fours, make sure you have everything you will be needing ready mixed and to hand. The accompanying ingredients would make an attractive and varied selection of petit fours riche.

Coat the sponge in a variety of the following ways:
Roll out some almond paste to $\frac{1}{16}$–$\frac{1}{8}$ inch thickness. Cut small rounds or squares of sponge and brush with apricot jam.
Cover completely and evenly with the almond paste. Dip each petit four into white or coloured glacé icing and/or pipe rosettes of butter icing all over with a very small star icing pipe.
Proceed as above but place a small additional almond paste shape on top of the petit fours before dipping into the glacé icing.
Spread the sides of squares of sponge with butter icing and roll in chopped almonds. Spread more butter icing on top and decorate.
Spread the side of ovals and rectangles of sponge with apricot jam. Roll out some almond paste. Spread the almond paste around the sides of the sponge, just coming over the top. Fill the top with glacé icing. Decorate.
Spread sponge shapes with apricot jam and coat with almond paste. Decorate the tops with a different coloured marzipan.
The variety of decoration is endless. Try to make as many shapes as possible, too—ovals, squares, trefoils, rectangles, crescents—but avoid star shapes, as they are too complicated.

Madeleines

| 1 quantity pâte genoise (see recipe page 119) | This is a classic French dish. Madeleine moulds are small shell-shaped tins.

Grease and flour some madeleine moulds (how many will depend on the size).
Fill the moulds ⅔ full with the prepared pâte genoise and bake in a moderate oven (350°F. Mark 4) for 7–10 minutes or until risen and golden. Cool on a wire rack.
Store in an airtight tin. |

Colettes

| 6½ oz. plain dark chocolate
1 oz. (2T) butter
2 teaspoons brandy, rum or sherry
4 tablespoons (⅜ cup) double (heavy) cream
flaked almonds for decoration

makes 16 | Chop the chocolate coarsely and put 4 oz. in a heatproof bowl or in the top of a double saucepan. Place over hot water and leave until the chocolate has melted. Using a teaspoon handle, smooth the chocolate over the inside of 16 small petit fours cases. Give each case 4 thin coatings. Allow to dry, then peel off the case and put the chocolate case in a fresh paper case.
Melt the remaining 2½ oz. chocolate using the same method as before. Beat the butter, allow to cool, then add the flavouring. Whip the cream lightly and fold in.
Allow the mixture to stand until it is of a piping consistency.
Using a large star icing pipe, pipe a large rosette into each prepared chocolate case. Decorate with flaked almonds. |

Macarons   Macaroons

| 6 oz. (scant 1 cup) castor (superfine) sugar
3 oz. (¾ cup) ground almonds
3 egg whites
split almonds
granulated (crystal) sugar | Macaroons, when made as for petit fours, are the classic accompaniment for ice cream.
Mix the castor (superfine) sugar and ground almonds together.
Whisk the egg whites until frothy, then use enough to bind the sugar and almonds together in a soft dough.
Pipe the mixture on to rice paper on a baking tray, with a plain icing pipe. The size will depend on how you wish to serve the macaroons. Petit fours size—about ¾–1 inch diameter rounds. Children's tea size 1½–2 inches diameter.
Place a split almond on each macaroon and sprinkle with granulated (crystal) sugar.
Bake in a moderately slow oven (325°F. Mark 3) for 20–40 minutes (according to size) or until pale golden in colour. Cool on a wire rack.

note: petit fours macaroons can be piped with a star icing pipe in fancy shapes, if desired. |

Cigarettes russes

| 2 egg whites
3½ oz. (½ cup) castor (superfine) sugar
1½ oz. (scant ½ cup) plain (all purpose) flour
1½ oz. (3T) butter, melted | These can also be served with ice cream.

Place the egg whites in a bowl and whisk them until they stand in stiff peaks. Add the sugar and sifted flour, mixing lightly, then the butter.
Grease and lightly flour a baking tray. Spread the mixture thinly on to the tray in rectangles about the size of a cigarette paper.
Bake in a hot oven (400°F. Mark 6) for 5–6 minutes.
Remove the rectangles from the baking tray, upside down, and quickly roll them around a pencil. Slide off and cool on a wire rack.
Store in an airtight tin.

note: the ends may be dipped in melted chocolate if desired. |

Meringues chantilly
Chantilly meringues

2 egg whites
pinch of salt
4 oz. (good ½ cup) castor (superfine) sugar
icing sugar
¼ pint (⅝ cup) double (heavy) cream
vanilla essence
flaked almonds for decoration (optional)

Place the egg whites and salt in a mixing bowl. Whisk until they are stiff enough to stand in peaks. Add half of the sugar and whisk until thoroughly blended. Fold in the remaining sugar with a metal spoon.
Grease a baking tray lightly, then dust it with a thin layer of flour. Tap the tray gently to spread the flour evenly. Pipe the meringue on to the prepared tray with a plain icing pipe. The size will depend on how the meringues are to be served, from the very small petit fours size to the large dessert size. Sprinkle generously with icing sugar. Bake in a very slow oven (200°F. Mark ¼) for 1–2 hours until firm and crisp but still uncoloured. Cool on a wire rack.
Whip the cream until firm, stir in the vanilla essence. Stick two meringues together with a teaspoon of cream. Serve decorated with flaked almonds if desired.

Gâteau jalousie aux poires et gingembre
Pear and ginger jalousie

8 oz. pâte feuillitée (see recipe page 119)
1 egg, beaten
2 large pears
2 oz. stem ginger (in syrup)

A jalousie can have many fillings, the simplest being jam. This recipe is particularly delicious.

Make the pâte feuillitée. Roll it out on a lightly floured board to form a rectangle 12 × 10 inches and about ¼ inch thick. Cut the pastry in half lengthwise to make two rectangles, each 12 × 5 inches. Trim a ¼ inch strip off each side of one rectangle, brush with egg and place on the top each side of the rectangle from which they were cut to make a rectangular 'flan case'. Place on a wet baking tray. Peel, core and slice the pears. Arrange the slices in the 'flan case'. Chop the ginger and scatter over the pears.
Fold the remaining pastry in half lengthwise. Starting ½ inch in from the end, and leaving a ½ inch border of pastry at the top, make cuts in the pastry along the folded edge at ¼ inch intervals. Open out, without letting the pastry stretch. Brush the 'flan case' edge with beaten egg and place the lid on top. Press the edges firmly together and knock them upwards with the back of a knife. Glaze the top with beaten egg and bake in a hot oven (425°F. Mark 7) for 20–25 minutes or until puffed up, crisp and golden.

serves 6   Serve as soon as possible.

Tuiles
Crisp almond biscuits

2 egg whites
4 oz. (good ½ cup) castor (superfine) sugar
2 oz. (½ cup) plain (all purpose) flour
1 oz. (¼ cup) ground almonds
2 oz. (4T) butter, melted
½ teaspoon vanilla essence

Place the egg whites in a mixing bowl, whisk until frothy, then add the sugar. Continue whisking until the sugar is mixed in. Add the sifted flour, ground almonds, melted butter and vanilla essence, stirring well.

Grease the required number of baking trays and place teaspoons of the mixture on them at well spaced intervals. Bake in a moderately hot oven (375 °F. Mark 5) for 5–6 minutes or until golden brown. Lift off the cooked biscuits and place them on a greased rolling pin to cool. Store in an airtight tin.

note: these biscuits can be served as petit fours or, if larger in size, as tea-time biscuits. The cooking time depends on the size of the biscuits made.

Gâteau pithiviers
Pithiviers cake

8 oz. pâte feuilletée (see recipe page 119)
2 oz. (4T) margarine or butter
2 oz. (good ¼ cup) castor (superfine) sugar
2 oz. (½ cup) ground almonds
1 egg, beaten
¼ teaspoon almond essence
1 teaspoon flour
apricot jam
extra egg for glazing
icing (confectionery) sugar

Pithiviers is a town in the Midi of France. This gâteau is a local speciality.

Roll out the prepared pastry on a lightly floured board to ¼ inch thickness. Cut out 2 × 6–7 inch rounds. Place 1 round on a damp baking tray. Roll the other out into a slightly larger round. Cream the butter and castor (superfine) sugar together in a mixing bowl, adding the ground almonds, egg, almond essence and flour. Beat the ingredients together thoroughly.

On the baking tray, spread the pastry with a little apricot jam, leaving a ½ inch border all round. Pile the almond mixture on top and make a dome shape. Brush the border with egg and place the second, slightly larger, round on top. Glaze the top with beaten egg, then slash curved cuts into the lid, starting at the centre, like the spokes of a wheel.

Bake in a very hot oven (450°F. Mark 8) for about 30 minutes or until well risen, cooked and golden. Cool on a wire rack.

serves 6 · Serve sprinkled with sifted icing (confectionery) sugar.

Palmiers

4 oz. (or scraps) pâte feuilletée
egg white
castor (superfine) sugar

Light crispy pastries which can often be made from left-over scraps of pâte feuilletée.

Roll out the prepared pastry, on a lightly floured board, to a thin oblong 12 inches in length. Trim the narrow ends, then brush with egg white and sprinkle liberally with castor (superfine) sugar.

Mark the centre of the oblong lightly with a knife (across the narrow part). Fold each half into 3, with the folds meeting in the middle. Fold the pastry in half and cut into ½ inch slices.

Place each pastry on a damp baking tray, leaving room for them to open out a little. Bake in a very hot oven (450°F. Mark 8) for about 10 minutes or until crisp and golden brown. Cool on a wire rack.

Sacristans

The ingredients for sacristans are the same as for palmiers (above) with the addition of a few chopped almonds.

The pastry is rolled thinly, then brushed with egg white and sprinkled with castor (superfine) sugar and chopped nuts. Press the nuts on firmly. Cut the dough into strips ½ inch wide and 3 inches long.

Twist each finger and place on a damp baking tray. Bake as above.

Chocolate cake

Tartelettes aux fruits Fruit pastries

1 lb. pâte sucrée (see recipe
page 119)
4 pears
juice of 1 lemon
12 black grapes
12 white grapes
6 oz. (¾ cup) apricot jam
glacé (candied) cherries
angelica (candied peel)

Make the pâte sucrée. Using only half of the pastry, roll it out
on a lightly floured board and line about 9 or 10 patty tins. Roll
out the remaining pastry and cut into thin strips about 10 inches
long and ½–¾ inch wide. Dampen each pastry strip with water and
wind up around a cream horn tin, wet side outside. Place small
rounds of greased greaseproof paper in the patty tins and fill each
with some baking beans. Place the cream horns on a baking tray.
Bake all the pastry cases and horns in a hot oven (400°F. Mark 6)
for about 20 minutes or until cooked and golden. Cool on a wire rack.
Peel, core and slice the pears thinly and dip each slice in lemon
juice to prevent discolouration. Halve and remove pips from the
grapes. Heat the apricot jam in a small saucepan, add the remaining
lemon juice, stir until the liquid is blended, then sieve. Fill the
cooked pastry cases with the prepared fruits, glaze the tops with
apricot glaze. Decorate with glacé (candied) cherries and angelica

makes about 14

(candied peel) and cut into small pieces.

Gâteau st honoré St. Honoré cake

1 quantity pâte à choux
8 oz. fresh strawberries
½ pint (1¼ cups) double
(heavy) cream
4 teaspoons gelatine
castor (superfine) sugar to taste
2 oz. (¼ cup) granulated
(crystal) sugar

Grease a 7 inch diameter ovenproof plate. Prepare the choux paste
and, using a large plain icing pipe, pipe circles on the plate from the
outside working inwards. Pipe the remaining mixture in small
mounds on a greased baking tray. Bake in a moderately hot oven
(375°F. Mark 5) allowing 40–45 minutes for the choux case and
20–30 minutes for the choux buns.
Prepare the strawberries, putting aside some of the best for
decoration. Press the remaining strawberries through a sieve to
make a purée. Mix the purée and the cream together and whip until
stiffened. Dissolve the gelatine in about 2 tablespoons hot water
and add to the strawberry cream with enough castor (superfine)
sugar to sweeten to taste. Leave in a cool place until almost set.
Place the granulated (crystal) sugar in a small saucepan with
4 tablespoons (good ¼ cup) water. Heat the saucepan, stirring until
the sugar is dissolved, then boil until a light caramel colour.
Dip each choux bun into the caramel and press around the rim of
the choux case, building up a high wall. Pour any remaining caramel
over the buns. Pour the strawberry cream into the middle of the
gâteau and leave to set. Decorate the top with the strawberries
set aside for the purpose, and serve as soon as possible.

note: the strawberries can be omitted and the buns filled with cream

serves 6–8

before they are built up into a tall cone shape on the choux case.

Choux aux fraises (ou framboises)
Strawberry (or raspberry) cream buns

1 quantity pâte à choux (see recipe page 119)
½ pint (1¼ cups) double (heavy) cream
1 lb. fresh or frozen strawberries (or raspberries)
icing (confectionery) sugar
makes 1 dozen

Put tablespoonsful of the prepared choux paste at intervals on a greased baking tray. Bake in a hot oven (400°F. Mark 6) for 30–35 minutes until well risen and golden brown.
Split each bun down one side and cool on a wire rack.
Whip the cream until stiff. Prepare the fruit. Pipe or spoon the cream into the buns and arrange the fruit on top. Dust each bun heavily with sifted icing (confectionery) sugar. Serve as soon as possible.

Savarin
Rum-soaked yeast cake

8 oz. (2 cups) plain (all purpose) flour
1 oz. fresh yeast or 1 tablespoon (1½T) dried yeast
6 tablespoons (½ cup) milk, warmed
½ teaspoon salt
1 oz. (2T) castor (superfine) sugar
4 eggs, beaten
4 oz. (8T) butter, softened
¼ pint (⅝ cup) fruit syrup or 4 oz. (½ cup granulated (crystal) sugar dissolved in ¼ pint (⅝ cup) water
3 tablespoons (¼ cup) rum or sherry
3 tablespoons (¼ cup) apricot jam
serves 6

Place 2 oz. (½ cup) of flour in a mixing bowl. Stir the yeast into the milk, add to the flour and beat well with a wooden spoon until it becomes a smooth batter. Allow to stand in a warm place until frothy, this will be about 20 minutes for fresh yeast and 30 minutes for dried yeast. Put the remaining 6 oz. (1½ cups) flour in a bowl with the salt, castor (superfine) sugar, eggs and butter. Add the yeast mixture and beat for 3–4 minutes.
Grease an 8 inch diameter ring mould (or two 6 inch diameter moulds) and half fill it with the dough. Cover the mould with a sheet of lightly greased polythene and allow the dough to rise in a warm place until the mould is ⅔ full. Bake in the centre of a hot oven (400°F. Mark 6) for 20 minutes.
Remove the savarin from the mould and place it on a serving plate. Heat the fruit juice with rum, sherry and pour over the savarin to soak it thoroughly. (Prick the savarin well with a skewer first to help the soaking). Cool.
Place the apricot jam in a small saucepan with 2 tablespoons (scant ¼ cup) water. Heat, stirring, until blended. Sieve. Glaze the savarin and fill with fruit as desired.

Savarin à la crème et oranges
Savarin with cream and oranges

Remove the peel and pith from 3 oranges and cut them into sections with a sharp knife, discarding all the skin. Keep on one side all the juice, squeeze the juice from one more orange and mix all the juice with 2 tablespoons rum. Use this syrup instead of fruit syrup to soak the savarin.
Keep aside the best orange segments for decoration, about 16–18. Chop the rest. Halve and remove the pips from 4 oz. grapes, keeping about 8 halves for decoration. Mix the chopped orange and the remaining grapes with ¼ pint (⅝ cup) whipped cream. Pile this mixture into the centre of the savarin. Decorate the top of the savarin with the fruit put on one side and about ¼ pint (⅝ cup) extra whipped cream, piped in rosettes.

Savarin aux pommes et caramel
Savarin with apples and caramel

Place 6 oz. (¾ cup) granulated (crystal) sugar in a small heavy pan and heat it gently until the sugar has caramelized into a rich golden brown. Meanwhile, halve and remove the pips of 4 oz. black grapes, remove the skin and pith from 2 small oranges and cut into segments, discarding all the skin. Core and chop 2 red-skinned dessert apples and dip in lemon juice to prevent discolouration. Mix the fruit together and pile into the centre of the fruit syrup and rum-soaked savarin. Dip small clusters of grapes into the caramel for decoration. Pour the remaining caramel over the savarin and arrange the caramel-dipped grape clusters around the edge.

Babas au rhum   Rum babas

1 oz. fresh yeast or 1 tablespoon
(1½T) dried yeast
6 tablespoons (½ cup)
milk, warmed
8 oz. (2 cups) plain (all
purpose) flour
½ teaspoon salt
1 oz. (2T)
castor sugar
4 eggs, beaten
4 oz. (8T) butter, softened
4 oz. (about ⅔ cup) currants
4 tablespoons (good ¼
cup) honey
rum to taste
3 tablespoons (¼ cup)
apricot jam
double (heavy) cream for serving
makes 16–17

Stir the yeast into the milk. Place 2 oz. (½ cup) flour into a mixing
bowl, add the milk and yeast and beat well with a wooden spoon
to a smooth batter. Allow to stand in a warm place until frothy.
This will be about 20 minutes for fresh yeast and 30 minutes for
dried. Put the remaining 6 oz. (1½ cups) flour into a bowl with the
salt, sugar, eggs, butter and currants. Add the yeast mixture.
Mix and beat well for 3–4 minutes.
Grease some dariole moulds (about 16 or 17 medium sized ones).
Half fill the moulds with the yeast mixture, cover with a sheet of
lightly greased polythene and allow to rise in a warm place until
the moulds are ⅔ full.
Bake at the top of a hot oven (400 °F. Mark 6) for 15–20 minutes.
Cool for a few minutes and then turn out on to a wire rack with a
tray underneath.
Place the honey in a small saucepan with 4 tablespoons (good ¼ cup)
water and rum to taste. Heat until blended and syrupy, stirring
constantly. Pour the syrup over the warm babas, soaking them
thoroughly.
Place the apricot jam in a small saucepan with 2 tablespoons (just
¼ cup) water.
Heat gently, stirring. Sieve. Brush the glaze generously over the
babas.
Cool, transfer to a serving plate and top with whipped cream.

Rum baba decorated with fruit

Croissants

1 lb. (4 cups) plain (all
purpose) flour
2 teaspoons salt
1 oz. (⅛ cup) lard
1 egg, beaten
1 oz. (good ¼ cup) fresh yeast or
1 tablespoon dried yeast plus 1
teaspoon castor sugar
6 oz. (12T) butter or margarine
extra egg for glazing
extra ½ teaspoon castor
(superfine) sugar

Mix the flour and salt, rub in the lard and stir in the egg. Blend
the fresh yeast into 7 fluid oz. (⅞ cup) water *or* mix the dried yeast
with 7 fluid oz. (⅞ cup) water plus 1 teaspoon castor (superfine)
sugar. Leave either for 10 minutes or until frothy. Add the yeast
mixture to the rubbed-in mixture. Mix well, then place on a lightly
floured board and knead the dough until smooth, 10–15 minutes.
Roll the dough out to a strip ¼ inch thick, 20 inches long and 8
inches wide, keeping the sides straight and the corners square.
Soften the butter with a knife, then divide into 3. Mark the dough
lightly into thirds, then dot the two-thirds with a third of the butter.
Fold the plain lower third up over the middle third and then fold the
top third down. Turn the dough a quarter turn to the left so that
the folds are to right and left. Press the edges lightly with a rolling
pin to seal them.
Roll out the dough again very gently by pressing the dough at
intervals with the rolling pin. Incorporate the other portions of
butter, separately, as before. Place the dough in a lightly greased
polythene bag and place in a cool place, preferably the refrigerator,
for 30 minutes. Roll out, as before, and repeat rolling and folding
3 more times. Leave in the refrigerator for a further 1 hour.
Roll out the dough into a rectangle about 23 inches long and 14
inches wide. Cover with lightly greased polythene and leave for
10 minutes. Trim with a knife to 21 inches and 12 inches wide.
Divide the dough in half lengthwise, then cut each strip into 6
triangles each 6 inches high with a 6 inch wide base.
Mix the extra egg with a little water and the extra pinch of sugar.
Brush the egg wash over each triangle and roll up, loosely finishing
at the point. Place the point underneath and curve the roll into a
crescent.
Place the shaped croissants on to an ungreased baking tray and
brush the tops with some egg wash. Place in a lightly greased
polythene bag and leave in a warm place for 20–30 minutes or until
puffed up. Brush with egg wash once more and bake in the centre
of a hot oven (425°F. Mark 7) for 20 minutes.
Serve warm.

makes 12

Brioche

½ oz. fresh yeast or 2 teaspoons
dried yeast plus ½ teaspoon
castor (superfine) sugar
8 oz. (2 cups) plain (all
purpose) flour
½ teaspoon salt
½ teaspoon castor
(superfine) sugar
2 eggs, beaten
2 oz. (4T) butter, melted and
cooled
extra egg for glazing
extra pinch of sugar

Stir the yeast into ½ tablespoon cold water; or, if dried yeast is
being used, mix the yeast and sugar together and sprinkle with
1¼ tablespoons water.
Using either method leave for 10 minutes in a warm place until
frothy. Sift the flour, salt and castor (superfine) sugar together. Add
the yeast liquid, eggs and butter and mix to a soft dough. Place on a
lightly floured board and knead well for about 5 minutes. Place the
dough in a lightly greased polythene bag and allow to rise in a warm
place for about 1–1½ hours.
Grease twelve 3 inch diameter brioche tins or deep bun tins. Divide
the dough into 12 equal pieces. Shape ¾ of each piece into a ball and
put into the tins. Press a hole firmly in the centre, then roll the
remaining ¼ of dough into a small ball and place it in the centre.
Put the filled tins on a baking tray. Put inside a large lightly
greased polythene bag and leave to rise until doubled in size, about
1 hour, in a warm place.
Mix an extra egg with pinch of salt and 1 tablespoon water. Brush
over the brioche and bake in the centre of a very hot oven (450°F.
Mark 8) for 10 minutes.

makes 12   Serve warm, with butter if desired.

Entertaining

The French people are hospitable and love to entertain. Whether it is a completely formal dinner party or merely a light luncheon on the beach, you can be sure that it will be beautifully prepared and served.

Further on in this chapter you will find some menu suggestions suitable for dinner parties. It is difficult, however, to go into menus for other occasions in such detail, since the dishes will rely so much on the occasion and the climate – whether the meal is to be eaten indoors or outside, and which foods are available at the time of year in your part of the world. After all, there is no such thing as a typical French menu; for instance, a Provençale menu would only very vaguely resemble a Breton menu or a Savoyard menu.

So select the recipes in this book which you feel would take in the above points but would also look attractive together when served according to variations in colour, texture and the main ingredients. It would be wrong to serve more than one cream dish or to present eggs or fish more than once. Serve a crisp light dish with a rich creamy one, checking that the finished dishes are not all of the same colour.

Serve French bread and butter as a matter of course, throughout the meal. If you are going to be very French, don't have side plates for the bread; your guests will just tear the bread into bite sized pieces on the table to their left. Always serve wine. The French are avid wine drinkers and it is the usual drink with everyday meals. Even the little children drink it, albeit with a little water added. Vin ordinaire is the everyday wine. The more important the occasion, the finer the wine to be served. Whether the wine is red or white, dry or sweet, will depend largely on yours or your guests' tastes. There are certain conventions which can be followed if in doubt (you will find these later on in the chapter) but the main thing is to enjoy the wine.

The wines of France

French wines are considered among the best, if not the best, in the world. Wherever vines are grown outside Europe, it is frequently French vines that are used and the wine produced is as near to its French counterpart as the vigneron can make it. Even wines made as far from France as Australia and America are still called Burgundys, Sauternes, Chablis and so on. It is impossible, though, to produce an exact imitation, because each year's grapes are slightly different and the taste and quality of a wine is affected by the weather and other natural factors such as the soil, local vegetation and the situation of the vineyard. On some wine labels you will now find the words 'appellation d'origine'. This ensures that the wine in that bottle actually came from the region after which it is named, e.g. Médoc.

You will find vines all over France with the exception of the extreme north. The most northerly vineyards are those in Champagne which produce grapes to make the inimitable sparkling wine of the same name. It is the fermentation process which makes the Champagne and, according to the amount of sugar added, the wine can be dry or sweet.

Bordeaux wines are among the best in France. The old vineyards produce a wine which has a good clear colour, a delicate bouquet and is smooth with a fine subtle flavour. The wines produced here are some of the most famous names such as

Red	White
Médoc, Margaux, Moulis, Listrac, Saint-Julien, Pauillac, Saint-Estèphe, Les Graves rouge, Saint-Emilion, Pomerol, Blayais, Canon et Côtes de Fronsac, Bourgeais, Côtes de Castillon.	Graves, Entre-Deux-Mers, Saint-Macaire, Haut-Benauge, Saint-Foy, Blaye et Bourg, Sauternes, Barsac, Cérons, Loupiac, St-Croix-du-Mont.

The Sud-Ouest and Bearn districts produce wines of mixed qualities. White, red, rose and sparkling wines are all made here. Some of the most famous are:

Red	Sparkling wines
Bergerac, Côtes de Duras, Pecharmant, Madiran	Gaillac, Rosé-Rosé de Bearn

White
Montravel, Bergerac, Rosette, Monbazillac, Jurançon

Burgundy is perhaps the most well-known wine growing area. Here they produce both red and white wines. The north of Burgundy makes fine dry white wine which is known as Chablis. Just south of this is the Côte de Nuits, which makes smooth velvety wines and is the home of the famous Nuits-St-George, Chambertin, Musigny, Clos de Vougeot, and so on. Again southwards, to the Côte de Beaune and such glowing wines as Corton, Pommard, Volnay and many more. The vineyards still stretch southwards through the Côte de Chalonnaise, Mâconnais and Beaujolais, producing, among many others, Pouilly-Fuissés, Montagny, and Chardonnay. In Beaujolais there are so many vineyards that each village has its own label. These wines are delicate and light with a rich bouquet. Some are very rough and need to be laid down to mature for some time before drinking.

Rhône wines have earned themselves an enviable reputation but those from the north are completely different from their southern counterparts. The white wines from the north are few but have an individual character. The better known wines are Condrieu, Chateau-Grillet, Hermitage and Saint Péray. The southern wines are varied in quality but the best are fine with a certain elegance. If drunk young, these wines are perfect when drunk with freshly

A typical pruned Grenach vine in the top terraces of Châteauneuf-du-Pape.

caught Mediterranean fish. The most famous are Laudun, Lirac and white Châteauneuf-du-Pape. Red Rhône wines again vary from north to south. The northern reds are full-bodied and robust with a high alcohol content. Red-Hermitage and Crozes-Hermitage are both rich red in colour, mellow and elegant. To the south, the red wines are lighter and more delicate although some have a powerful aroma and bouquet. The most famed is Châteauneuf-du-Pape, which is traditionally served with game, especially venison. Rosé wines are also produced in this area, the best of which come from Chusclan, Lirac and Tulan. A few fruity dessert wines also come from the Rhône valley.

Provence produces a variety of wines white, red and rose. The vineyards stretch along the Mediterranean coast and inland as far as Aix-en-Provence. Although some are exported, such as Cassis, Bandol, Bellet de Nice and Palatte d'Aix, the majority of wines are drunk locally as they are the perfect partner to Provençale food.

Alsace. The character of Alsace wines has made them famous throughout the world. Mainly white wines are produced and they are rich in bouquet. Who does not know these familiar names, Riesling, Traminer, Gewurztraminer, Tokay and Muscatel?

Jura and **Savoy** wines are not too well-known outside of France. Jura wines can be white or rosé and are well-balanced, fruity but delicate. They are at their best when laid down or placed in barrels to mature for a long time. Savoy wines are fresh and light. They are at their best when served with lake or river trout in the Savoy. White, red and rosé wines are all produced here.

The **Loire** Valley is noted for its vineyards which stretch for miles either side of the river. The sweet white wines of Anjou are famous

The vineyards of Gigondas (Department Vaucluse) which produce one of the appellation controlée Côtes-du-Rhone-Villages wines.

Wine taster from Provençe.

for their smoothness and fruitiness. Coteaux de Layon, Aubance, Bonnezeaux and Savennières are just a few of the better known. Vouvray, Montlouis, Saumer and Touraine are the names of just a few of the sparkling and semi-sparkling wines produced in the Loire valley. Muscadet is a well-known local dry white wine. This area is also just becoming recognised for its rosé wines, especially those from Anjou and Touraine. Red wines are in the minority here although some very good ones are made such as the light red Chinon and Bourgeuil.

Languedoc Roussillon in the south of France is the home of the simple table wines. Vin ordinaire, which every household in France drinks, mainly comes from here as this wine can be drunk very young and does not have to be pampered. Dry white wines such as Languedoc 'Clairettes' and Bellegarde, red wines such as Corbières, Minervois, Fitou and St George d'Orques and sparkling wine such as Blanquette de Limoux are famous throughout France although not so well-known outside the country. Many of the sweet natural dessert wines such as Muscatel and some fortified wines are also from this area.

Choosing and serving wines

Generally, the more you pay for a bottle of wine, the superior the quality—but this is not always so. It would be an advantage if you could find out the quality of the vintage year in which the wine was made. Sometimes a poor vintage year produces only a limited crop of grapes and therefore only a limited number of bottles of wine. On the other hand a good vintage year, producing a really superb wine, may also coincide with a good crop and therefore more than enough bottles which can be sold at a reasonable price. Whatever its quality, the wine must be cool to touch, sealed (preferably with a cork) and a good clear colour.

It is as well to know what food is to be eaten with the wine. You may have your own ideas as to which wines you prefer—and why not, as this is definitely a matter of personal taste and the main idea is to enjoy your wine? If, however, you are giving a dinner party and would like to serve the correct wines with each course, you may find the following suggestions helpful:

Hors d'oeuvres	Dry or medium dry white wines.
Fish and shellfish	Dry white wines; dry white sparkling wines.
Poultry	White or red dry and rich in bouquet but not too full-bodied.
Meat	Red wine, dry and not too fullbodied.
Game	A full-bodied, rich and generous red wine.
Cheeses	Serve a full-bodied good vintage red wine with strong cheeses. A lighter dry white wine should be served with mild and soft cheeses.
Desserts and fresh fruit	Champagne; sweet sparkling and still wines; sweet dessert wines.

Champagne is the only wine that can correctly be served throughout a meal. At some time before it is to be drunk, make sure that the wine will be the correct temperature at the time of serving. White and rosé wines should be served chilled but not iced. Sweet white wines should be even cooler. Place the bottle in the refrigerator for at least 1 hour or until the wine is sufficiently cool. Sparkling wines should be served slightly chilled; if possible

138

the bottle should be placed in a bucket of ice for a while before serving. Red wines should be served at room temperature and the bottle should be opened about half an hour before the wine is to be drunk. Never try to alter the temperature of wine quickly; it should be a slow, gradual process so as not to spoil the wine.

To my mind, wine tastes good out of any glass, but if you have gone out of your way to obtain a good quality (and probably expensive) wine, it is well worthwhile serving it in the correctly shaped glass. Only use uncoloured glasses which will show off the colour and clearness of the wine. Generally speaking, only half fill a wine glass, as this will enable the full bouquet of the wine to rise and be appreciated before the actual wine is sampled. This is especially true of red wines which are generally served in rounded glasses to stop the bouquet from escaping. For a full dinner party you will probably need four glasses on the table for each person: one for dry white wine, one for red, one for sweet white and the last for sparkling wines or Champagne. They will also be placed on the table in that order, since light and white wines are generally served before full-bodied and red wines—excepting, of course, the wines served with the dessert and fruit.

Dinner parties in the French manner

When the French entertain, they can produce anything from a full eight course dinner party (for very special occasions) to the simplest of cold picnics. Either way, care is lavished on each dish and great attention is paid to the serving.

A complete dinner for a special occasion can still be the same elaborate type of banquet which was frequently given in the last century. The various courses would be as follows:

Hors d'oeuvres	Appetizers.
Potage	Soup.
Poisson	Fish
Entrée	Meat dish made in an elaborate manner.
Relevé	Joint of meat.
Rôti	Roast game or poultry.
Entremet	This is a vegetable, a sweet, and an after dinner savoury or cheese.
Dessert	Fresh fruit, petit fours or small ice cream.
Café	Coffee.

A suitable menu for such a splendid dinner (if you feel that you could cope) might be:

Pamplemousse au Gingembre	medium dry or sweet white wine
Crème de Concombre	dry or medium dry white wine
Sole à la Colbert	dry white wine
Tournados au Poivre	dry red wine
Rôti de Porc	dry red wine
Poulet Rôti au Beurre	dry red wine
Choufleur Polonaise	dry red wine
Diables à Cheval	dry red wine
Mousse au Chocolat	sweet white wine
Poires Bourguignonne	sweet white wine
Café	liqueurs

139

It is usual today to omit various courses in order to simplify the menu: omit either the soup or the hors d'oeuvres and only serve one dish of meat or poultry. The entremet consists of a vegetable dish and a savoury, while the sweet entremet is often coupled with the dessert. An hors d'oeuvres is served as well as soup when it is a fish soup and the fish course is not served.

Menu 1

Hors d'oeuvres varié	medium dry white wine
Truites Amandine	dry white wine
Poulet à la Marengo	dry red wine
Haricots Vertes au Beurre	dry red wine
Diablotine Gruyère	dry red wine
Chartreuse de Fraises	sweet white wine
Café	liqueurs

Menu 2

Consommé	dry sherry or white wine
Sole Normande	dry white wine
Cote d'Agneau à la Bretonne	dry red wine
Pomme de Terre à la Lyonnaise	dry red wine
Fromage	full-bodied dry red wine or light dry white wine according to the cheese
Poires Belle Hélène	sweet white wine
Café	liqueurs

Menu 3

Avocat Vinaigrette	medium dry white wine
Bisque de Homard	dry white wine
Chateaubriand	dry red wine
Pommes Château	
Courgettes aux Amandes	dry red wine
Aigrettes au Fromage	dry red wine
Soufflé au Citron	sweet white wine
Café	liqueurs

Menu 4

Salade de Tomate	medium dry white wine
La Bourride	dry white wine
Carré de Porc Provençale	dry red wine
Pommes Mousseline Provençale	dry red wine
Crème au Camembert	light white dry wine
Fruits	sweet white wine
Café	liqueurs

By carefully planning your menu according to the occasion, you can lengthen or shorten the meal by adding or subtracting a course. Bear in mind the character of the meal: rich, expensive dishes may be included, as in menu 3, or a more economical and less formal meal planned as in menu 4. The peasant dishes are not meant to be included in a dinner party menu and I would suggest that you try them on your family, since they are a delicious and ideal way to cook a whole dinner in one pot, without all the added trimmings.

Weights and measures

All recipes in this book are based on Imperial weights and measures, with American equivalents in parenthesis.

Measures in weight in the Imperial and American systems are the same. Measures in volume are different, and the following table shows the equivalents:

spoon measures: level spoon measurements are used throughout the book.

imperial	american
1 teaspoon (5 ml)	$1\frac{1}{4}$ teaspoons
1 tablespoon (20 ml)	$1\frac{1}{4}$ tablespoons (abbrev.: T)

liquid measures:

imperial	american	
20 fluid oz.	16 fluid oz.	1 pint
10 fluid oz.	8 fluid oz.	1 cup

Metric measures

The following table shows both an exact conversion from Imperial to metric measures and the recommended working equivalent.

weight:

imperial oz.	metric grams	working equivalent grams
1	28·35	25
2	56·7	50
4	113·4	100
8	226·8	200
12	340·2	300
1·01 lb.	453	400
1·1 lb.	$\frac{1}{2}$ kilo	
2·2 lb.	1 kilo	

liquid measures:

imperial	exact conversion	working equivalent
$\frac{1}{4}$ pint (1 gill)	142 millilitres	150 ml.
$\frac{1}{2}$ pint	284 ml.	300 ml.
1 pint	568 ml.	600 ml.
$1\frac{3}{4}$ pints	994 ml.	1 litre

linear measures:

1 inch	$2\frac{1}{2}$ cm.
2 inch	5 cm.
3 inch	$7\frac{1}{2}$ cm.
6 inch	15 cm.

It is useful to note for easy reference that: 1 kilogramme (1000 grammes) = 2·2 lb. therefore $\frac{1}{2}$ kilo (500 grammes) = roughly = 1 lb. 1 litre roughly = $1\frac{3}{4}$ imperial pints therefore $\frac{1}{2}$ litre roughly = imperial pints

Oven temperatures

In this book oven temperatures are given in degrees Fahrenheit with the equivalent Gas mark number. The following chart gives the conversions from degrees Fahrenheit to degrees Centigrade:

°F	°C	
225	110	very cool or very slow
250	130	
275	140	cool or slow
300	150	————
325	170	very moderate
350	180	moderate
375	190	moderately hot
400	200	
425	220	hot
450	230	very hot
475	240	

Index

Figures in italics refer to illustrations

143

Acknowledgements

The following colour photographs are by courtesy of:

Birds Eye Lobster Bisque (p. 11); Salmon Trout in Aspic (p. 14); Trout with Almonds (p. 56); Beef cooked in Burgundy Wine (p. 65); Chicken with White Wine and Mushrooms (p. 80) **Colman's Mustard (Martin Chaffer)** Camembert cream (p. 95) **Egg Board** Cheese Omelette (p. 11); Veal Loaf (p. 15); Prawn Butter Balls (p. 56); Crêpes Suzettes (p. 116) **Food from France (Sopexa)** A selection of locally produced French food (p. 6); A selection of French Cheeses (p. 10); Provençale Fish Stew (p. 56); Coq au vin (p. 77); Jugged Hare (p. 86) **Fruit Producers Council** Pork Chops in Cider (p. 72); Chicken with Apples and Cider (p. 82); Chicken and Pear Vol-au-Vent (p. 83); Savarin (p. 113); Apple Charlotte (p. 116); Flaming Apples (p. 116); Apple Flan (p. 117); Empress Rice (p. 117); Burgundy apples and pears (p. 117); Fruit Pastries (p. 125); Chantilly Cream Cake (p. 125) **Herring Industry Board** Herrings Brittany-style (p. 49); **Jif Lemon (Martin Chaffer)** Red Mullet with Garlic and Herbs (p. 57); **John Lee** A selection of pastries and apple flan (p. 2–3); **John West** Tuna Fish Provençale (p. 10); Pineapple Nut Shortcake (p. 124) **Kraft** Peach Cake (p. 121); Chocolate Cake (p. 128) **New Zealand Lamb** Loin of Lamb with Haricot Beans (p. 64) **Paf International Christian Délu** Scallops Breton-style (p. 11); Meat served with White Sauce (p. 15); Stuffed Ham Rolls (p. 68); Duck with Orange (p. 83); Snow Eggs (p. 116) **Potato Marketing Board** Potatoes with Cheese (p. 91) **Rapho** Pâtes (p. 10); Preparing meat (p. 61); Cold Meat and Relishes (p. 73); Stuffed Tomatoes and Ratatouille (p. 87); Onions used in Cooking (p. 90) **RHM Foods** Quiche Lorraine (p. 10); Veal Stew (p. 76); Mushroom Soufflé (p. 94)

The following black and white photographs are by courtesy of:

Angel Studio Dressed Crab (p. 55) **Argentine National Meat Board** Tournedos à la Béarnaise (p. 64); Stuffed aubergines Provençale (p. 92) **Birds Eye** Sole Fillets served with Sauce Veloute (p. 19) **British Egg Information Service** Sauce Mornay added to Eggs Florentine (p. 16); Eggs Lorraine (p. 38); Cooking an Omelette (2 steps) (p. 42); Making a Soufflé (5 steps) (p. 43); Savoury Eclairs (p. 99); Chocolate Mousse (p. 102); Apricot Soufflé Omelette (p. 104); Charlotte Russe (p. 107); Lemon Soufflé (p. 112); Chantilly Meringues (p. 127); Strawberry Cream Buns (p. 130) **Conway Picture Library** French Onion Soup (p. 33); Preparing leeks for Cold Leek Soup (p. 34); Chopping leeks for Cold Leek Soup (p. 34) **Eden Vale** Yoghourt Orange Sorbet (p. 102); Cream Hearts (p. 109) **Flour Advisory Bureau** Quiche Lorraine (p. 44); Raspberry Pancakes (p. 101); Rum Baba decorated with Fruit (p. 132); Croissants (p. 133) **Findus** Mediterranean Vegetable Stew (p. 4); Plaice Fillets in Cheese Sauce (p. 48); Fillets of Sole Orly (p. 50) **Food from France (Sopexa)** French Cheeses (p. 96) **Fruit Producers Council** Pears with Ice Cream and Chocolate Sauce (p. 22); Apple and Orange Flan (p. 114) **Gale's Honey** Honeyed Peaches (p. 111) **Heinz** Choux buns with Fruit Sauce (p. 22); Ham Mousse (p. 23); Lamb Cutlets (p. 71); Mediterranean Vegetable Stew (p. 92); Genoese Sponge (p. 120) **Paf International** A selection of French dishes (p. 134) **Rapho** A selection of Egg dishes (p. 36) **Syndication International** Genoise Sponge in preparation (p. 12); Spooning half-set Aspic over Veal Galantine (p. 27); Cold Leek Soup (p. 34); Trout with Almonds (p. 46); Fillet of Beef in Pastry served cold (p. 67); Savoury eclairs in preparation (p. 99); Filling Savoury eclairs (p. 99); Cream Caramel (p. 106); Crêpes Suzette (p. 108) **Van Den Berghs** Chocolate Flan (p. 103); St. Honoré Cake (p. 118) **Wine Board** Wine used in cooking (p. 9); Pruned Grenach Vine (p. 136); The Vineyards of Gigondas (p. 137); Wine Taster from Provençe (p. 138)

   PDO 81-604